iX LEADERSHIP:
CREATE HIGH-FIVE CULTURES AND GUIDE TRANSFORMATION

BY
DR. RACHEL MK HEADLEY & MEG MANKE

with Michelle Stampe

Find Your Way Press
Spearfish, South Dakota

for Alex, Jobie, and Peyton —

our first dreams come true

that made us believe all others are possible

FOREWORD

As America's workforce shifts from Baby Boomers to Millennials, our attitudes toward culture have shifted along with it. While Baby Boomers were content to not upset the apple cart, Millennials said, "To hell with the apples and the cart," and built their own. They value culture as much as, if not more than, salary and benefits. How a company is led plays an integral role in how they will decide where they want to work.

As Millennials change the expectations of the modern workforce, companies need to change the way they promote their culture—not just to attract good workers, but to retain them, too. Everyone wants to hire the best and sometimes they do, but how long will they stay? This is just one example of how iX Leadership relates to one of my mantras, "Adapt, change or die." A company that refuses to change risks getting left behind and, frankly, going out of business. Changing company culture can seem hard, but it's necessary to keep the right kind of employee.

When I met Meg and Rachel through the Hero Club, a Council of the C-Suite Network, I realized right away that they get what other leaders don't. They understand that the key to a bomb-proof company isn't some streamline initiative or budget strategy. It's not insanely expensive benefits packages or an employee gym—it's culture. It's the kind of culture that motivates employees to "show up" for their company.

Business owners need to learn how to lead employees who can help evangelize their culture and brand. These are your "ambassadors." They may not always be the loudest people in the room—but being a leader means seeing something in someone that other people don't. Your ambassadors will be your biggest advocates because they subscribe to your vision; therefore, they embrace your mission.

So, what destroys culture and sends good employees running? When leadership stops communicating. While it's tempting to deploy stop-gaps when communication breaks down, in the long run, it'll lead to more chaos and confusion. A company needs a common language, relatable core values, and a clear vision. Everyone in the company needs to share that vision—from the CEO down to the mailman.

If business owners want to create a strong, lasting organizational structure that helps employees become their best ambassadors, leaders need to lead by example. Whether you're a multi-million-dollar enterprise or a brick and mortar store, your employees will look to you as the example. Every leader must be able to reflect a company's values and should exemplify them every single time. But don't try to copy someone else's culture as your own. It'll make you come across as a phony, and no one likes that. Authenticity is what culture is all about.

This book will show you how to do just that. Meg and Rachel know people, and they know leadership. This book holds the secret to creating a culture that increases productivity, generates good employees, and fosters a creative environment where people actually want to work. This is a culture that easily adapts to the highly-competitive, volatile business climate that challenges organizations today. This book belongs in your hands if you want to become the kind of leader that inspires every employee to be their organization's biggest ambassador. That's iX Leadership.

BOOYAH!

Jeffrey W. Hayzlett

Primetime TV & Radio Host, Speaker, Author and Part-Time Cowboy

To boldly go where no man has gone before

A scientist and a cowgirl walk into a bar…

…they talk to the ownership team, and revenue goes up by 10x.

Meg Manke (cowgirl) is a human resource executive turned senior partner in Rose Group International (RGI), a consultancy that specializes in designing exceptional Internal Experience (iX) for organizations.

She's been riding horses and rounding up cattle on the High Plains of South Dakota since she was five. She loves her people, but is quick to let you know when you're not holding up your end of the deal. She is passionately committed to education and improving the lives of others. She's been told to bring the energy back a notch (tone it down!), but her quick mind and big heart guide the development of organizations and their leadership to incredible new heights.

Meg has always loved business, leadership, and strategy. And Sci-Fi.

Dr. Rachel MK Headley (satellite scientist) loves to diagnose really thorny root-cause issues and create action-based solutions. She works with Meg as a senior partner in RGI.

She is a big-picture thinker who loves people, and can get seemingly impossible things done—which can sometimes surprise her Mensa brethren. She always wanted to be an astronaut and staged an end-around into the space industry through her work as an operational science officer for the Landsat satellite mission.

Today, she takes the lessons she's learned from working with big budgets and global missions to build high-achieving teams and develop iX Leaders.

Problem: Rampant disengagement of the workforce has led to poor corporate performance.

The focus on individual leadership accomplishment has led to a lack of team and culture development.

There is this crazy pervasive notion that work and change has to suck.

Yeah, we know. Most corporations have created environments where work and change do suck.

But, imagine a different scenario.

As a leader: Your team values your role and believes in you. You feel connected to the leadership team, and know they are transparent about what's going on in all areas of the organization. You understand, value, and relate to the company's core values and vision and are proud to be associated with them. You can communicate with the people around you (above and below) and can convey exciting and challenging news with equal skill.

As an employee: Your team leader appreciates you. Your teammates believe in you. They have your back. You have theirs. You get what the company is about, and you like being associated with it. The senior leadership feels connected to your job and gets what it takes to do it. As things constantly change, you know why things are happening, how long it will take, and who's being affected. You know you can raise a hand to ask a question or make a suggestion without getting it chopped off.

Every leader should be 1.) developing, seeking, and building High-Five Cultures. And, since high-intensity is the hallmark of business, every leader should be 2.) guiding their team through transformations. These are the most critical skills for today's leaders.

Most leaders don't have a clue how to do either of these things well.

iX Leadership integrates these two skills into core tenets of leadership. Instilling iX Leadership in your corporation solves the problem of rampant disengagement, which leads to corporate success. Through a healthy dose of psychology, leadership strategy, and personal anecdotes, we'll show iX Leaders how to implement change, create a culture of innovation, and inspire powerful teams to produce.

After all, without our people, we are nothing.

Disclaimer:

In iX Leadership *we engage in honest conversations full-heartedly with salty language and tough-love.*

Are you ready? Let's talk.

- *Meg and Rachel*

CONTENTS

PART I
DISCOVER

G.S.D.

"We are experts in Get Shit Done."

Dr. Rachel MK Headley
Senior Partner & Culture Strategist, Rose Group Int'l

Four adventurists hop into a canoe in the middle of nowhere…

Each of four friends are one of the four Culture Types: Fixer (Fred), Independent (Isabelle), Stabilizer (Sam), and an Organizer (Olivia) (oh my!).

These four friends plan to spend a week canoeing through the Boundary Waters in Minnesota. They've planned one of those trips that the outdoor community calls "second-hand fun"—so arduous that it's only enjoyable when remembered from the comfort of their soft couches months later (We personally do not subscribe to this type of fun, although we do get talked into it occasionally).

They plan to wind their way through dozens of miles of pristine backcountry, carry their canoes over steep rocky portages, and sleep on remote islands adorned with Native American pictographs. It is a serious undertaking for novice paddlers, as the remote landscape of the Minnesota-Canada border is one of the few wilderness areas left where engines are not allowed on the water or in the sky. As their first paddle strokes hit the clear, cold water of Fall Lake, there is a feeling of excitement, nervousness, and possibility.

The first few days of the trip sail by. Everyone is in a good mood, laughing off blisters and soaking up the late May sun. The fish are biting, and the wind is blowing just hard enough to keep the mosquitoes away. Everyone is optimistic.

Day three is a different story. What was a gentle breeze has become a stiff headwind that pushes against them as they try to paddle forward. That night, it's cold—colder than they anticipated or planned for. At 7 a.m., the frost on their sleeping bags has just started to melt. Fred and Sam find fabric scattered on the forest floor and trace little strands of nylon and polyester back to their packs. *Damned chipmunks.* Their only food aside from what they catch has been ransacked. Last night everyone vowed to never eat Northern Pike again—or any fish, for that matter. Morale is low, and they are cold, sore, and hungry. Their hands are blistered through their gloves, and they can't seem to stay dry in the chilly spring drizzle. What's more, Sam twisted his ankle yesterday. This morning it's swollen and sore. They are at least 20 miles from cellphone reception and their launch site (and their Subie, which will drive them to an all-you-can-eat China Buffet on their first day off the water).

Isabelle, always one for a change of plans, looks at the group and says, "Let's change our route and head east today."

Olivia and Sam look at each other, skeptical.

Isabelle continues, explaining "the loop around Basswood lake will add an extra day to our trip, but if we continue to fight this headwind it might add three. If we take the longer route, the wind will be at our back and we will end up getting home faster."

Olivia looks at the map. "We haven't charted out any of that route, we have no idea what to expect. We could be heading into a current that is coming the opposite way. I think we should stick to our original route. The headwind might lessen up, and at least this way we know where we're going."

Isabelle sighs, and continues to argue her point. Exasperated, Sam turns to Fred and asks, "What do you think?"

Fred looks around the fire, considering what each choice would mean for every member in the group. He looks at Sam's puffy ankle, and knows he can't keep hauling the heavy canoes over the portages. However, he also knows that Sam and Olivia won't want to change the route without doing a little research first.

Fred remarks, "Let's go west. We can't finish our route in six days at this pace, and even without the headwind, we can't sustain another 20 miles of paddling. If we go west and loop around Pipestone Bay, we'll cut our trip short, but then we can see the pictographs, skip a few portages, and will be back to shore on schedule."

All three look at Fred, clearly unpersuaded. He says, "It will be a minor change, we were going to head through there anyway. Think of it as a shortcut, rather than a reroute." He turns his head toward Isabelle. "This way you can for sure see the pictographs you were so excited about."

Olivia looks at Sam. "How much is your ankle going to slow us down?"

"It's not! I'm okay." Sam wasn't about to be the person who *ruined* the entire trip by taking a shortcut. He was willing to suffer it out for his friends.

Isabelle says, "We definitely can't stay here. I still think we should go east. The wind will be pushing at our backs, and we'll get even more out of our trip."

"We have no idea what to expect east or west, let's just stick to the plan," Olivia interjects. "This is what we all agreed on when we started, and it still makes the most sense."

"No, it doesn't. We can't keep paddling in this wind—"

"The wind will probably clear up or just switch direction anyways! We need to stick to the route we originally chose!"

(Wait, is this the premise of *The Blair Witch Project*?)

Does the conversation above sound familiar? Sometimes a discussion devolves into a game of tether ball, with each participant pounding the same point over and over again back at the other person. Everyone ends up restating an argument or statistic already discussed ten minutes earlier, and everybody leaves the conversation wondering if anyone else heard anything they said.

These kinds of zero-sum arguments happen all the time in business (and in life). Leadership is then left to figure out how to keep their team from a full-on battle royale. Later in the book we'll circle back to this disagreement and show you how this kind of interaction can become something constructive rather than explosive.

If the dialogue between the adventurists feels familiar for you or your team, you aren't alone.

Almost 200 million articles pop up from a Google search on "team dynamics." These articles describe every challenge regarding people in your business. They address disagreements of every flavor and bad behavior of every stripe. They talk about poor productivity, low sales, disengagement, customer service issues, underperformance, turnover and low retention, too much ego, not enough ego, resistance to change, and on and on.

While these articles cover a wide range of topics, they all share a common issue: they aren't listing causes; they are listing *symptoms*.

What's the root cause?

Poor corporate culture.

The solution? iX Leadership.

iX Leadership is a new leadership approach that focuses on the Internal Experience (iX) of your people. The greatest leaders will all tell you that they can't achieve anything without their teams, and we're going to show you how to get the very best out of your team consistently and easily through improved company culture.

Part I of this book will introduce an entirely new typology: Culture Types. Culture Types are a framework upon which to stratify your team based on how they like to work. Culture Types allow you to best leverage the energy of your people. We developed Culture Types from the same research that gave rise to personality assessments like Myers-Briggs Type Indicator ® and DiSC ®, with one major caveat. Culture Types are designed for today's business environment, which means they focus on teamwork and constant change.

Part II will examine how people move through changes. Whether a team is transitioning into a new office space or a new industry, they will react in predictable ways. Psychologists have been studying the U-shaped curve indicative of a transition for decades (here's a hint: our model isn't U-shaped). The Kurtz Change Transition Model (KCTM) shows you how to inspire innovation in your teams. That's right—change sparks innovation. The changes leaders routinely make their teams "suffer through" are the very things that create highly engaged teams. Most leaders regularly *throw away* the opportunity to cultivate what they seek most in their people: creativity.

Part III uses the new ideas in the first two sections to refine classic (and critical!) leadership techniques. It is filled with stories that exemplify how to better interpret and use 'nothing-new-under-the-sun' leadership skills with the help of Culture Types and the KCTM.

iX Leadership isn't only the most effective way of leading people, it will change the way you see the world. Take a moment to consider the *Internal Experience* (iX) of your organization. When your team walks through the front door of the office, do they feel excitement or dread? Is your team energized, or apathetic? What's playing over the loudspeaker? A *Star Wars* John William's score, or a tormenting Wagner opera? Does your team look forward to coming into work on Monday?

Do you?

Peering through the lens of a company's iX impacts everything—from qualitative data like sales, budget, deadlines, retention, productivity, and profit—to the nuanced stuff, like optics, leadership, and company culture. iX gives insight into the team experience, such as to what degree employees feel valued, autonomous, innovative, and satisfied. Another way to measure iX is by analyzing the energy of a team. Do they go the extra mile because they want to? Are they challenged? Motivated?

It's ironic that the tools necessary to build a strong iX are commonly called "soft skills," considering the Navy SEALS argue that teamwork is on the same platform as "mental toughness." Whatever language a person uses, one this is clear: a strong iX is synonymous with a strong organization, and that kind of power begins with teamwork.

Many organizations, big and small, are starting to pay attention to their iX. Caterpillar, worth $47 billion, experienced a staggering $8.8 million in annual savings with a 70 percent increase in productivity when they focused on their iX. They also boasted a 34 percent increase in customer satisfaction and significant drops in absenteeism, turnover, and overtime. Since their success, they have made company culture their top priority in every location.

When HK Metalcraft Manufacturing Corp., a family-run-turned-big-business metal house started to focus on culture, they began to see results. They reaped the benefits of improved communication channels, heightened employee morale, a goal-oriented workforce, and ultimately, a happier team. That translated into serious dollars. After the transition, HK Metalcraft retained $700,000 in sales, enjoyed a return of $150,000, and as a result of new products and processes, achieved a cost saving of $50,000.

A company doesn't have to be as big as Caterpillar (or HK Metalcraft, for that matter) to see results. Whether a company has four team members or 4,000, focusing on company culture will dramatically impact its bottom line.

Influential organizations like the Navy SEALS can't be successful without high-performing teams that are challenged, driven, and inspired by leadership to reach their full potential. A strong team will propel any organization infinitely further than any budget strategy, any streamline initiative, or any reorganization. When managed correctly, the quality, quantity, and value of teamwork will exponentially increase.

The problem is, few organizations can create the environment necessary to get the very best out of their teams. Honestly, they rarely experience second-or third-best. A recent Gallup study shows that out of America's 100 million full-time employees, only a mere 33 percent report liking their job. One-third of the population actually likes going to work. Fifty-one percent of 100 million employees are disengaged at work. Over half the workforce is "just getting by."

These are the employees that do the bare minimum until 4:00 p.m. and ultimately don't care how well the company performs (so long as they continue to have a paycheck, like Peter Gibbons and his friends in *Office Space*).

So, if 33 percent of employees are happy and 51 percent are apathetic, what's going on with the other 16 percent? These employees are *actively disengaged* in the workplace. An actively disengaged team member spends most of their day on Facebook. Despite knowing they could perform better, they choose not to because they hate their company, their boss, and their job. When these employees leave the office, they grab a beer with their friends and describe loudly and in detail to what extent they don't want to go to work in the morning.

> **Peter Gibbons:** The thing is, Bob, it's not that I'm lazy, it's that I just don't care.
> **Bob Porter:** Don't…don't care?
> **Peter Gibbons:** It's a problem of motivation, all right? Now if I work my ass off and Initech ships a few extra units, I don't see another dime, so where's the motivation? And here's something else, Bob: I have eight different bosses right now.
> **Bob Slydell:** I beg your pardon?
> **Peter Gibbons:** Eight bosses.
> **Bob Slydell:** Eight?
> **Peter Gibbons:** Eight, Bob. So that means that when I make a mistake, I have eight different people coming by to tell me about it. That's my only real motivation is not to be hassled, that and the fear of losing my job. But you know, Bob, that will only make someone work just hard enough not to get fired.
>
> *Office Space, 1999*

Additionally, the average adult will spend 35 percent of their total waking hours at work. When that data is combined with the statistics from Gallup, it appears that 67 million Americans will spend around 95,000 hours of their life "just getting by." If most Americans are unfulfilled in their working life, then the condition of the modern workforce is in a crisis.

It's tempting for leadership to shrug their shoulders and say, "that's not my problem." However, choosing to be blind to employee dissatisfaction is like entering a race with a broken leg. If your team doesn't care, you may as well forfeit—you've already lost. You've lost because disengagement is expensive. These employees take more time off, are less productive, make more mistakes, and wreak havoc on optics from a P.R. perspective.

Disengagement is particularly expensive when a company goes through a tumultuous time, such as a change initiative or reorganization. Employees who hate their jobs are not going to stay loyal during a transition. While a company can't buy loyalty, they pay for not having it. Society for Human Resource Management (SHRM) predicts that every time a business replaces a salaried employee, it costs six to nine months' salary on average. For a manager making $60,000 a year, that's $30,000 to $45,000 in recruiting and training expenses.

A CAP study found that this rate is related to salary. For example, an organization can expect to pay more based on employee compensation, as seen below:

- 16 percent of annual salary for high-turnover, low-paying jobs (earning under $30,000 a year). The cost of replacing a $12/per hour employee is about $4,150.

- 20 percent of annual salary for midrange positions (earning $30,000 to $50,000 a year). The cost of replacing a $40,000 manager is $8,000.

- Up to 213 percent of annual salary for highly educated executive positions. For example, the cost of replacing a $1 million CEO is $213,000.

Consider the expense of hiring a new employee. Costs include finding qualified applicants (such as advertising, screening, and interviewing) and don't forget the cost of onboarding a new person, including time taken from management to train. Then there is the cost of loss in productivity as well as the dip in sales resulting from poor customer service (as you're well aware, new people are prone to errors and slowness). Finally, consider the cultural impact the loss of an employee has on an organization.

What unsuccessful leaders fail to see—no, choose to ignore—is their own ability and responsibility to orchestrate an environment where employees can find meaning in their work.

Companies with disengaged employees have missed the opportunity to create a culture where work becomes discipline, repetition becomes skill, and challenge becomes its own reward. They've overlooked that coveted space of ingenuity, innovation, and creativity—where the line between "have to" and "want to" blurs into "get to."

Not only is this oversight a travesty regarding profitability, but also regarding ethics. Committed leaders inspire their employees to become their best selves. Not just a version of "good enough," but a version of themselves that they never thought possible. Strong leaders value their team—as a resource, an investment, and as people.

Think of iX Leadership as a roadmap to reunite leaders with the rest of their team. Our mission is to revolutionize the way leadership views and leverages the energy of their most valuable asset: their people. We create company culture in which each member of a team has the freedom to be innovative, the drive to be productive, the motivation to hold themselves accountable, and the opportunity to be proud of the work they have accomplished. It is a culture that doesn't just meet the bottom line, but one that continuously exceeds it.

iX Leadership is not handholding—we don't do group hugs. We deliver. We maintain that weak company culture has poorly utilized, undervalued, and bored employees who aren't inspired to achieve much of anything, let alone their full potential. Through our expertise, experience, and case studies of major companies employing hundreds of employees, we have seen firsthand what a strong iX can do. When teams are managed in a way that optimizes their best qualities, companies become more profitable, every time.

This book isn't the first leadership book to answer the question, "why does company culture matter?" Actually, most leadership books tackle the *why*. They explain why a positive company culture boosts profitability and creates high-performing teams. *iX Leadership* is different in that it answers *how*: it not only provides the tools to create a strong *Internal Experience*, but the manual as well. It reveals how to inspire a team to step into their best selves by bolstering the positive aspects of a team's unique dynamic.

Furthermore, *iX Leadership* acts as a guide to cultivating a company culture that can handle any change. While every organization is one-of-a-kind, we've seen the same story over and over—the people leading the organization have a higher tolerance for change than the teams they oversee. In general, 44 percent of people in an organization resist change due to lack of information or understanding, while 38 percent dislike the change (we argue that's because they don't understand the reasoning behind it). For the first time, in *iX Leadership,* a change approach combines leadership values with an individual's tolerance for change to create a positive *Internal Experience*.

THE 8 STEPS OF iX LEADERSHIP

"Tools are wonderful, if you know how to use them."

Meg Manke
Senior Partner & Culture Expert, Rose Group Int'l

- Know who you have on your team (Culture Types): Part I

- Know how your people deal with change (KCTM): Part II

- Know how Culture Types affect change transitions: Part II

- Get your mindset on (iX Perspective): Introduction

- Know and live your Values: Part III

- Know and communicate your Vision: Part III

- Know how Accountability and Empathy are sisters: Part III

- Become an iX Ambassador and Change the World

CULTURE TYPES

Rachel's Take:
Raise of hands: Who has felt like a misfit before? I know I have.

My first job in satellite science was one of those positions where someone tells you what to do and when to do it. It was a "these are your duties, now do them" culture, which was fine by me at the time. I needed rules and instruction—I didn't know what to do, how to do it, or when to ask questions. I didn't even know what questions to ask yet. I was delighted to have a roadmap.

As time went on and I became more adept at the role, I began to come up with all kinds of ideas to improve their process. I wanted to help make things more streamlined and efficient. From my perspective, I sought improvement and innovation, but that wasn't how the company saw it. From their perspective, I was trying to change an institution that didn't need to be changed. I was not in a position or an organization where new ideas were readily implemented, especially when those ideas came from the mouth of a young scientist. Stifled, I ended up leaving the project.

As I now know, I was a Culture Type mismatch. I am a Fixer, and I was operating in an Organizer role. This worked for a time, but it was not a long-term solution *for me*. It is critical to understand that an Organizer who could do that job, and do it incredibly well, isn't a better team member than me. It's just that I was ill-fitted to that role.

Once we are cognizant of our gut-response to change with respect to group dynamics, we gain a more objective perspective of ourselves, becoming aware that as unique as we may be, we still act in a predictable way. As a team member in an organization, once you identify your pattern you learn to honor it by managing situations in which you find yourself ill-suited. As an iX Leader, understanding Culture Types means predicting how others will respond to different roles. Leaders can then use that knowledge to design an iX where their people find themselves in the right role, the first time.

Do you prefer to be adaptable or organized?

Is it more important to make a decision or to gain buy-in?

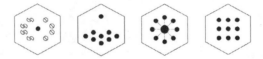

How We're Different

By answering those two questions, we can place you in one of our four Culture Types. For a more precise result, take our online survey at:

https://rosegroupintl.com/the-quiz/

A perceptive leader already values company culture. They may have already taken a step toward tailoring their leadership style by identifying their own personality profile through systems like Myers-Briggs Type Indicator® or DiSC®; they may have even completed the 34-aspect StrengthsFinder® or found their color through the Color Code®. These personality profiles offer leaders insights to their own quirks and habits, as well as those of their teammates. From there, a leader can discern with whom they work best and by whom they will be challenged.

Here's the problem: while personality profiles are informative and useful on a personal level, they have failed to translate into *real* results for the organizations that use them. Part of the issue with personality profiles is that they orient to the individual. For example, let's say that you've just taken a Myers-Briggs Type Indicator® test and have found that you are an ENTP (like Meg!) or an ENTJ (like Rachel!). While you may find it fascinating that you are 7 percent more extroverted than the average person or that your dominant preference for perception is intuition, that information is only valuable on an individual level and doesn't offer a simple explanation as to how you work on a team. That's problematic considering teamwork comprises of 80 percent of the average work day of an employee.

Furthermore, personality profiles are too complicated to use in a group setting. For example, when we sit down to have a conversation, there is only one channel of communication. Meg – Rachel. With a single communication channel, it's easy to apply the significance of our individual personality types to the conversation. We can both communicate effectively while simultaneously considering the relevance of each other's personality.

Then our writer (another ENTP) pops through the door. Now, we have three people with three lines of communication. Meg – Rachel, Meg – Michelle, Rachel – Michelle. It's getting tough to keep track of who's who, but still manageable. However, once our graphic designer comes through the door and adds a fourth person, we are suddenly in the midst of *six* communication channels.

> For you Organizers, the equation is:
> communication channels =
> number in your team x (number in your team - 1) / 2.
> For a team of 8:
> communication channels = 8 x (8-1) / 2
> communication channels = 8 x (7) / 2
> communication channels = 56 / 2
> communication channels = 28

Considering most of us work in teams more than three individuals, it's not surprising that personality profiling doesn't produce results in an organizational setting. With personality profiling, it's nearly impossible to keep track of who is who, and what significance that holds in any given situation.

Another issue with personality profiles is that they are packed with information. Some assessments present over 20 detailed pages describing how a person processes data, makes decisions, and communicates with others. The sheer density and quantity of information supplied makes it impractical to sift through every page to find one or two critical components to work on and then put it into practice. The DiSC® assessment even offers certain levels of each personality component, demonstrating even *more* specificity. How can a leader remember that they themselves are a high-D, middling-C, with a low S and i, let alone that Jerry from accounting is a middling-D and low-C?

Furthermore, only portions of the lengthy report provided are relevant to a work environment. Does it ultimately matter, from an organizational context, that April from data acquisitions is likely to struggle in her romantic relationships because she is a natural debater or that Frank has a deep and powerful connection with nature? Sure, it's interesting, but again, it's not *useful*.

The third issue is one of applicability. What problems can be answered with the personality assessments? They can offer insight into personal challenges, but to what end? Most assessments agree that you can behave in a way that is outside your core traits, but that people rarely change their personality. When they do, it is usually a consequence of a negative experience, like a severe concussion or a traumatic event.

So then, if we can't change our personality, what do we actually gain from an awareness of it? In our experience, personality profiling leads to excuses, not solutions. We've heard countless people use the personality profile as a crutch, arguing "I'm an introvert, so I can't be asked to speak during meetings," or, "I'm a Yellow, so I can't be expected to finish projects." What was intended to bring out the strengths of each team member has ultimately turned into a lack of accountability.

Our typology—Culture Types—differs significantly from this paradigm. Culture Types don't measure personality directly. Within our four categories and two axes of measurement, a person can be introverted or extroverted, judging or perceiving, or feeling or thinking. They can be genuine, shallow, humble, or egotistical. Instead, Culture Types are designed to shed light on behaviors that can predict the type of work you enjoy and the structure of the work environment in which you excel.

Culture Types do not assign value to any given Type. We have actively avoided "good" or "bad" labeling. Consider what has happened to the labels "introvert" and "extrovert" since the popularity of personality assessments. Many people made implicit (and explicit) assumptions that extroverts make the best leaders. Then in 2012, Susan Cain wrote *Quiet: The Power of Introverts in a World That*

Can't Stop Talking, and since then websites like Inc., The Huffington Post, and Psychology Today can't wait to tell readers why extroverts are superficial while introverts are deep, mysterious thinkers. Misguided interpretations have the propensity to devolve from their original intent to be repackaged as the trend of the week.

Culture Typing isn't meant to organize people into different careers. All Types are lawyers, poets, artists, entrepreneurs, and scientists. They are all leaders and team members at different points in their lives. However, the way in which they approach their career is something we do measure. We can predict how they lead and follow, what kind of work environment gets them excited, and what kind of leadership style leaves them energized. We will even show leadership how to tailor job descriptions to different Culture Types to get the right fit and show applicants how to discern whether or not they are applying for a job they will enjoy.

Culture Typing takes the labor out of job sculpting. While it would be wonderful to have the time and resources to tailor every role to every member of a team, that isn't a realistic goal. However, it is realistic to place team members in one role or another based on their Type. It is also realistic to tailor a position to one of four Types, as opposed to the myriad of individual personalities and preferences that make up an organization. Culture Typing is a practical and pragmatic job sculpting tool.

Culture Typing frees leadership from the arduous task of figuring out how to manage multiple generations. Instead of worrying over how to pair a Millennial with a Baby-Boomer, leadership can focus on the Culture Type of individuals on the team. Culture Typing is a much more accurate way to facilitate teamwork as opposed to generational assumptions. Furthermore, because all four Culture Types are represented in every generation, a leader can feel confident that their assessment is free of age-based biases.

No single Culture Type is best suited for leadership. Every Type has strengths and preferences, and understanding Culture Types is about understanding the value that each brings to an organization. There are influential leaders who are flung out to the very corners of our Cartesian graph, acting out every stereotypical trait of their own Culture Type; as well as those hovering near the center, acting as chameleons, changing their colors as needed. There are successful leaders that, by some centrifugal force, reside on each point of each axis, living in perpetual *chaos* or continuous *order,* consumed in *self* or immersed in *team*. Ideally, a good leader recognizes when and how to draw from every category, despite where they tend to land on the graph.

The names of each Culture Type are intentionally descriptive and intuitive so that leadership can take the information in this book and start applying it in their team right away. For example, Fixers tend to fix problems, Independents tend to act independently, Organizers tend to organize, and Stabilizers tend to create stability. Of course, that doesn't mean that an Independent can't be organized or that a Fixer is doomed to a life void of any stability. Anyone and everyone, usually on a day-to-day basis, acts independently, organizes something to some degree, fixes a problem, and creates a stable environment. What trait or traits a person chooses to demonstrate at any given moment in time is heavily influenced by the situation. However, while behavior is fluid and non-prescriptive, Culture Types are designed to identify what is most natural, or where a person feels most at home. Even though everyone can learn to act like another Type with practice and intention, it isn't generally a long-term option.

Finally, Culture Types are simple to use. Having only four categories and two axes of measurement, an iX Leader can start applying the information in their teams right away. It doesn't matter if a team is made of three people or 3,000—Culture Types are streamlined enough to integrate into every size of organization.

Culture Typing measures two things, and two things only: a person's tolerance for chaos and how they operate in a team environment. Consider these metrics while forming generalizations about each Type, and before applying them outside of their original context. While Culture Types transcend the world of business, they are not designed to be a clinical diagnosis for one's personal life: Culture Types are neither prescriptive or rigid. They do present a new lens with which to view the world, but a limited one. We intentionally put limits on our Typing so that its intended use is a methodical approach to understanding and altering the nuances of team dynamics, especially in the face of change.

Once we identify your Culture Type, we can answer questions to better place you in the right role, such as: What kind of a team structure do you prefer? What kind of roles within that group do you enjoy? What are you challenged by at work, and what do you excel at? How quickly do you recover from transitions (both predicted and unexpected)? Do you like change? When are you most creative, and how can you become more creative in the future?

If you are a leader, Culture Types will give you a light-bulb insight to not only your own preferences, but also those of your team. You'll begin to understand why some individuals respond well to your style, while driving others crazy. It will become obvious why some of your team members exasperate you by dragging their feet, while others are eager to brainstorm. Culture Typing answers complex questions about your team, such as: Why are some people more engaged in a team than others? Who wants control over the big-picture, and who wants control over the details? Who is better suited for what roles within an organization? What is the best strategy for getting a team on board with a new initiative? It will become apparent why you may or may not have a higher tolerance for change than the rest of your team, and why it seems like it takes so long for the rest of your organization to hop on board with a new idea.

As an iX Leader, you can use this information to shape your own company culture. This is a culture with a clear vision that is supported by a high-performing team driven by innovation and transformative change. This is a work culture that boasts remarkable customer service, increased retention, improved productivity, dedicated employees, and an unrelenting team.

This is *your* team, with a strong iX.

If you haven't yet taken our quiz, we encourage you to take a few minutes now to do so. Knowing your Type will give you some context as you begin to relate the information here into your own team, organization, and worldview.

https://rosegroupintl.com/the-quiz/

Our Culture Typology is based on two factors that have been converted into *x* and *y* axes:

X-axis: Are you driven by a team environment, or do you prefer to work alone? Our *X-axis* measures Team – Self.

Y-axis: Do you prefer order or chaos? Our *Y-axis* measures Order – Chaos.

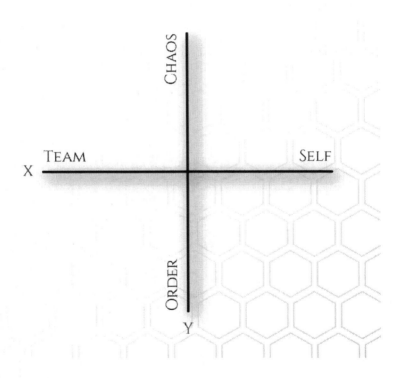

Because our system is built on two axes, we can generally Type someone by the first two questions in the chapter. Here they are again:

Do you prefer to be adaptable or organized?
Is it more important to make a decision or to gain buy-in?

Types who land in either quadrant above the *x-axis* are *chaos-tolerant*, meaning that they prefer a dynamic environment and are comfortable with the unexpected. Those who fall below the *x-axis* are *order-tolerant*, and therefore flourish under routine and prefer parameters. Types scoring to the left of the *y-axis* are *team-driven*, meaning they are aware of group dynamics and love building consensus. Types scoring to the right of the *y-axis* are *self-driven*, indicating they orient to the individual (themselves) before orienting to the group.

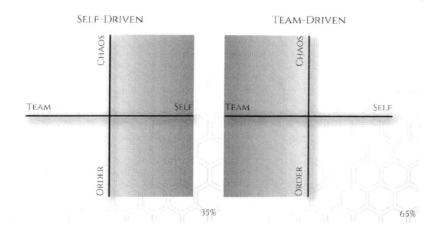

SELF-DRIVEN

CHAOS

TEAM — SELF

ORDER

35%

TEAM-DRIVEN

CHAOS

TEAM — SELF

ORDER

65%

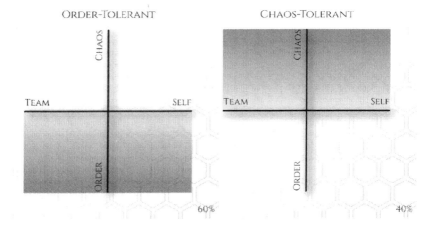

ORDER-TOLERANT

CHAOS

TEAM — SELF

ORDER

60%

CHAOS-TOLERANT

CHAOS

TEAM — SELF

ORDER

40%

We have labeled each quadrant in a manner that best describes the overlapping characteristics of each axis:

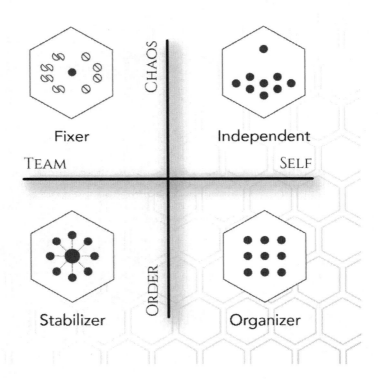

STABILIZERS

Team + Order

DRIVERS

- To operate within social and order
- To have stability
- To have security
- To create cohesiveness
- To be a part of something
- To have time to process information
- To have confidence in their surroundings

FEARS

- To be alone
- To be judged
- To not have a plan
- To be in opposition to others
- To be left out or ignored
- To do something incorrectly
- To stand out from the crowd or go against others

Stabilizers are driven by *team* and *order*. They are deeply interested in others and prefer structure in their environment. They make up about 43 percent of the population, making them by far the most common Culture Type. Stabilizers are the foundation of an organization, not only because they are the majority, but because they act as an anchor. Stabilizers are solid—unwavering, steady, reliable. If put in the right position, they will show up every single day, on time, and do an incredible job within their realm of expertise. Stabilizers both seek and create security and certainty.

 **Preferences**

Stabilizers are all about order. They want to know what they are supposed to do and when they are supposed to it. They thrive under strict rules, concise language, clear parameters, and daily routines. They like to have control over the small details of projects and are incredibly adept when it comes to precision.

Stabilizers' preference for order makes them very detail-oriented. They are unlikely to forget something important or make mistakes in tedious roles. They also like to know the details of any given situation. They want to know what's happening, why it's happening, and how it will affect them.

Stabilizers prefer to blend in, and are rarely disruptive unless absolutely necessary. When there is work to be done, Stabilizers buckle down and grind it out. Stabilizers' propensity to create order out of chaos makes them fond of rules, both formalized regulations and social norms. However, a Stabilizer might be inclined to break the rules if it is socially acceptable to do so. For example, a Stabilizer might speed on a busy stretch of road because "everyone speeds through there." Alternatively, they may feel comfortable walking down Main Street covered in tattoos with a spiked up mohawk—so long as their social group looks and acts somewhat similar.

 ## On a Team

Stabilizers play an integral role in team dynamics—they are the lifeblood of a strong team. They have an incredible drive and ability to keep everyone tracking toward a unified goal. They are inspired by the idea of working together to achieve a common vision. When there is a disagreement, they are often the unifiers.

Stabilizers prefer to work with others and value their co-workers immensely. Stabilizers are acutely aware that success is a team effort and realize their own area of expertise is only one piece (as integral as it may be) of an entire production. They are incredibly perceptive as to what their role is in relation to others, and they easily integrate into most team dynamics.

Because Stabilizers are reliable, they tend to stick with projects until the very end. Once they commit to doing something, they follow through with it. They want to know exactly what's going on, exactly what success looks like, and exactly where they fit into the project. Once shown how to get something done, a Stabilizer will continue to do it efficiently every day, every time.

Stabilizers aren't as effective on a team when they are forced to stand out. Standing out might include working on individual assignments or being put into any situation where they have to be contentious. Stabilizers actively avoid making unpopular decisions because they hold the opinions of their teammates in such high regard. Stabilizers don't readily offer critique or criticism, especially if doing so would inconvenience or hurt another person.

 ## In Leadership

We call Stabilizer leaders "eye of the storm" leaders. During changes, transitions, or periods of innovation, these leaders create sanity out of insanity by gathering the team into the eye of the hurricane while the wind rages around them. In the face of adversity, Stabilizer leaders protect the team above all else.

Stabilizer leaders are generally quite popular. Their group orientation paired with their reluctance to implement changes that are unwarranted or unpopular make them well-liked by those they manage. Because 60 percent of people are *order-tolerant* and 65 percent are *team-driven*, these leaders have an easy time identifying with the majority of their team. When Stabilizer leaders do implement changes, it is after a lot of serious consideration, and implementation is slow and controlled.

Stabilizer leaders thrive in industries that require a "right" way to do things. These leaders can be trusted when extreme safety or discipline is needed. We see Stabilizer leaders in organizations that range from NASA to the U.S. Army, and in industries from manufacturing to environmental, and from health to safety.

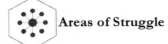

Areas of Struggle

Stabilizers may struggle to see the value in analyzing new options. If the methods or practices in current use are "good enough," a Stabilizer will keep them that way. Stabilizers also have a hard time seeing benefit in ideas that aren't quite finished baking in the oven. That's because those ideas are generally not yet supported with much detail or by the rest of the team. In other words, Stabilizers aren't interested in ideas that answer *why*; they want the answer to *how*.

Although Stabilizers are brilliant problem solvers in their specific area of expertise, they do not intuitively carry those skills into unfamiliar areas. That's because solving problems that have a multifaceted or undefined scope involves potentially compounding Change Events, which can feel very chaotic. As we've mentioned, that isn't exactly a Stabilizer's wheelhouse. Stabilizers are less effective in roles where they *continuously* have to solve problems that are outside of their comfort zone or that put them at odds with the rest of the group.

Because the antithesis of stability is change, they generally have a difficult time with transitions. Ask a deep Stabilizer (a Stabilizer who scored far from the center and the axes of our graph) how they feel about change, and they'll say, "Oh, I *hate* change!" Any dramatic change (what we call a Change Event), such as a reorganization, career switch, or even an office relocation is stressful for Stabilizers. It can take a Stabilizer a very, very long time to accept and then familiarize a change. It's not because they walk around thinking "change is bad!" (although they might!), it's because they are protecting the familiar, and thus accepted, way of doing things.

A Stabilizer's popularity can come at a high cost. We've found that *team-driven* Types, especially Stabilizers, are sometimes so aware and concerned with others that they wind up in a gossip spin or, as Meg puts it, a soap opera. Furthermore, Stabilizers don't always perform well on projects or roles where they feel isolated or at odds with the rest of the team. They generally dislike any role that involves administering performance reviews or "lessons learned" synopses.

Stabilizer leaders can fall into the trap of making the easiest decision because of their preference for what is familiar. For example, a Stabilizer leader might keep a problematic employee on the team or continue to use the wrong software because that's the way it's always been. These leaders can have a difficult time pulling the trigger on anything that will be divisive or lead to confrontation, even when they are confident it is the right call. Without proper training, these leaders can struggle in volatile industries that demand constant adaptation.

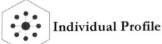 **Individual Profile**

Everyone's favorite neighbor, Fred "Mister" Rogers, was likely a Stabilizer. No surprise there—most Stabilizer leaders are very popular with their team. Fred Rogers had a deep preference for order, which can be seen in his repetitive style of "Mister Rogers' Neighborhood." For decades, every episode begins and ends in the same way. The camera pans slowly over his neighborhood, as the "neighborhood trolley" crosses a few streets as the viewer zooms into Mister Rodger's set house. Mister Rogers steps inside, whistling his famous song, "Won't you be my Neighbor?" as he hangs up his jacket and puts on his iconic sweater (which was knitted by his mom). At the end of every episode, Mister Rogers always said the exact same line: "You always make each day a special day. You know how: By just your being you. There's only one person in the whole world that's like you, and that's you. And people can like you just exactly the way you are. I'll be back next time. Bye-bye!" His meticulousness and strict attention to the little things (like which shoes to wear on set), are undeniably *order-tolerant* traits, and undeniably what made his show such a success.

Stabilizers often make excellent communicators. Fred Rogers was no exception. Not only did he have an incredible gift for translating big ideas into material suitable for children (in one episode Mister Rogers deals with the death of his pet fish), but he was also adept at communicating with adults. When President Nixon proposed cutting the PBS budget in half, Fred Rogers testified before a Senate subcommittee. Chairman John Pastore had never even seen his show. Fred Rogers was so convincing that Pastore ended up giving PBS $22 million, *increasing* the PBS budget by $2 million.

Fred Rogers, like many Stabilizer leaders, was willing to go to bat for his team. His fight to secure funding for PBS ensured that his team, America's children, would continue to have a resource that would set them up to become good citizens. His life was devoted to their future, and in that way his life was devoted to his team.

Meg's Take:

During my first year at Creighton University, the business school only provided the four traditional business majors: finance, accounting, economics, and marketing. Yes Millennials, business schools traditionally only offered four majors. While I was a student, the professor teaching business ethics, Dr. Beverly Kracher, decided business ethics ought to be an entire major. She set off on the uphill journey to make it happen (which would be a major transition for a Jesuit University, mind you).

Through diligence, patience, and hard work, Dr. Kracher single-handedly paved out a business ethics major. Today, Dr. Kracher is the endowed chair of business ethics professors at Creighton University and has created the Business Ethics Alliance, which is an organization in Omaha where people pay a membership and network and learn about business ethics.

FIXERS

Team + Chaos

DRIVERS

- To operate within social and chaos
- To improve
- To be helpful
- To be flexible and adaptable
- To achieve expert mastery
- To have control over their environment
- To realize a vision with the help of others

FEARS

- To be mediocre
- To hurt others
- To feel compressed
- To feel regimented
- To be micro-managed
- To be perceived as ineffectual or weak
- To create unintended negative consequences

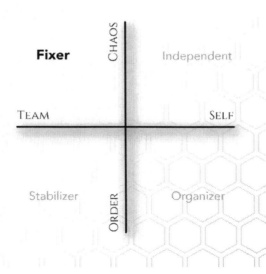

Fixers make up a little less than a quarter of the population at 22 percent. They are driven by *team* and *chaos*.

The term "fixer" has also been used to identify covert problem-solvers that discreetly clean up a mess for their clients (Mike Ehrmantraut in *Breaking Bad* and "The Wolf" in *Pulp Fiction* may come to mind). Our Fixer name stems from the same root: to fix things; to take care of problems. As their name implies, Fixers are *de facto* problem solvers. They interpret roadblocks and curveballs as opportunities to brainstorm a solution. That isn't to say that other Culture Types can't solve problems, but Fixers innately and automatically begin solving issues before they even arise. They are masters of "what-ifs" and contingency plans.

Fixers are interested in people—who they are, what their story is, and how they are impacted by change. We don't mean to suggest that all Fixers are bleeding hearts and caregivers—what we mean is that Fixers are aware of how their actions and the actions of others impact each other and the work. Often, but not always, this awareness manifests in a desire to focus on a common good, to help others, and to offer support. Fixers are generally quick to lend a helping hand—they hate to be seen as lazy or ineffectual. A Fixer rarely stands on the sideline.

Preferences

Fixers relish change because it gives them an opportunity to solve problems. For a Fixer, a change is a chance to see things in a new light, and from a new perspective. For example, if they are working on a problem they are quick to think, "This approach isn't working, let me try out something new." Fixers believe that failure is integral to learning (Stabilizers and Organizers don't see the world with this logic, generally speaking).

Change is what allows Fixers to be innovative, creative, and spontaneous. If something isn't right, they will try bold or original methods to make it right—as long as the end result benefits the whole. If something can't be fixed, they will throw it out altogether and instead search for the perfect solution. They'll move from career to career, seeking just the right fit; or they'll move from location to location, finding a place that meets all of their needs. "Suffering through" or "gutting it out" is not a viable long-term option for a Fixer. In some contexts, Fixers can be seen as the ultimate perfectionists (Stabilizers can see them as constantly meddling).

Fixers prefer a little chaos, or as a Fixer might say, a "less structured" environment. For Fixers, chaos is synonymous with freedom, and freedom is the ability to get creative. In order to innovate, Fixers need a little room to breathe, and can easily feel constrained by rules or authority. While a Fixer is quick to understand why some sort of structure is necessary to avoid problems, they feel constricted by rules and regulations that they perceive as outdated, ineffectual, or unnecessary. Fixers loathe arbitrary rules (LOATHE).

Fixers aren't usually detail-oriented people. Unlike Stabilizers, who like to know exactly where they fit and what their role looks like, Fixers enjoy a little more fluidity. Generally, when an issue is brought to their attention they drop everything and fix it. They won't ask very many clarifying questions—they don't want to get bogged down by specifics, and instead tend to focus on the big picture. They'll ask, "What does the end result look like?" They may or may not stick around to hear the answer.

Fixers don't mind challenging the status quo if they deem it necessary to fix a problem—they aren't easily intimidated by the chaos that will likely result from a poorly managed change. However, a Fixer isn't going to open a dam to watch water career down a canyon. Fixers tend only to disrupt a social structure if there is a *problem* with it. Why fix something that isn't broken? Why inconvenience others without a reason to do so? Fixers weigh a potential solution against the energy it will take to support the team. Is the juice worth the squeeze?

On a Team

Like Stabilizers, Fixers are team players. They love working in a group, and often have the mentality of, 'we all fail together or succeed together.' When Fixers begin to problem solve, they seriously weigh the opinions, preferences, and knowledge of the entire group to form a singular, unified solution. While they can be hasty, Fixers often weigh the consequences and implications of any change and strive to create an environment that serves every party involved, if possible.

Fixers prefer to work with a team in a role where they are free to make decisions and implement changes. They can't stand when something isn't right, and therefore want the power and freedom to be able to make corrections where they see fit. When thrown a new project they usually jump on board right away, already figuring out what needs to be done before reading the entire memo.

Fixers tend to avoid working by themselves. They can go off and fix a problem, especially if it's over a relatively short duration, but they prefer to work with a group if given the opportunity. A Fixer won't function at their highest level unless they are in an environment that facilitates collaboration.

In Leadership

Fixers are problem-solving leaders. They are the leaders that are most likely to leave their office and actively seek out problems and find solutions for their team. These leaders continuously seek out ways to make their organization more innovative and effective. They'll walk the floor, ask people how their day is going, and see if there is a way they can make their work day better.

Fixer leaders genuinely appreciate their team and know that if they go the extra mile for their people, the sentiment will be returned ten-fold. Because of their team-based mindset, these leaders value the opinion of their team and will often ask them for ideas and input. Fixer leaders enjoy building consensus and gaining buy-in.

Fixer leaders are rarely accused of being afraid to make tough decisions, as long as they are confident those decisions will be in the team's best interest. Because they are *chaos-tolerant*, they can handle the potential blow-back from unpopular decisions. Of course, being team players means they are hesitant to implement a change they deem unwarranted. These leaders consider the consequences of change before pulling the trigger. They want to know who it will affect and to what degree before throwing a massive unknown onto another person's plate. They have the ability to be incredibly conscientious in this way. Whether it's because Fixer leaders know that upsetting their team will only create more problems to fix or if it's due to their social awareness, they are intentional about the way in which they affect others.

Fixer leaders excel in dynamic leadership roles that lack a "how-to" section and demand flexibility. They are not only willing, but are eager to hop in the trenches with their team. Therefore, these leaders are found in volatile roles where they work closely with their people. We see Fixers in companies from Uber to Apple.

Areas of Struggle

Fixers tend to be less effective when they go to work and do the same thing every day. They don't adjust to repetitive tasks and can feel constrained if their daily routine is too rigid. We see Fixers get "burnt out" in roles with little variation, and will rarely stay the course in these roles.

Fixers don't like being told what to do. That's because they want control over their environment, and therefore can easily feel micromanaged. They can operate in a role with strict parameters over a short duration if they realize it is essential for the project or for the rest of the group, but over time it will wear on them.

Fixers can be accused of having a 30,000-foot view, meaning that they are so concerned with the big-picture they forget about the detail (or completely ignore it). They get halfway into a project, realize they've neglected to pay attention to critical information, and are forced to go back and fix a problem they've created. In other words, Fixers start making decisions and creating solutions before they have the whole story. Fixers will dive headfirst, only to realize mid-dive they're headed into the kiddy pool. As our Fixer editor keenly pointed out, "our tendency to work things out in advance can quickly devolve into worst-case-scenario thinking, bordering on obsessive neuroticism…especially under stress." This kind of mentality can further exacerbate the problem (which, as he can attest, is nothing to say for what it does for the individual's sanity).

Forgetting to "look before you leap" can not only increase the timeframe of a project, but can also annoy team members. Fixers are often accused of fixing things that aren't broken, while exasperating their *order-tolerant* teammates in the process. Sometimes their effort to fix something is driven by a desire for gratification. When they change something that doesn't need to be altered and their efforts are ignored, they can feel slighted and unappreciated.

Fixer leaders run into problems when they start implementing too many changes too quickly. They will roll out ten new initiatives with the desire to help their team, only to throw their *order-tolerant* team members into a state of total anxiety and frustration. When put in this situation, we hear *order-tolerant* Types say things like, "before I have a chance to wrap my mind around something, she changes it, *again*."

Individual Profile

Christa McAuliffe stepped on board the Challenger on a brisk morning in January 1986. She was prepared to give the lesson of a lifetime. As the first civilian prepared to enter space, McAuliffe was making history. Tragically, McAuliffe never left the atmosphere: she and six other crew members died 73 seconds into their mission as the Challenger disintegrated over the Atlantic Ocean.

"Today, I'm directing NASA to begin its search, in all of our elementary and secondary schools, and to choose as the first citizen passenger in the history of our space program, one of America's finest, a teacher." When President Regan called upon America's school teachers for the opportunity of a lifetime, 12,000 teachers applied to experience space travel onboard the Challenger. For NASA, Christa McAuliffe was the obvious choice. She was smart, tenacious, passionate about space travel, and incredibly dedicated to her students. For Fixer Christa McAuliffe, being the first nonscientist in space would be the answer to a major problem in the world.

As a history teacher, McAuliffe saw a lack of social history (history of the common person) not only as unfair, but as a demotivator in her classroom. She felt like her students didn't understand that regular people comprise history, saying, "I would like to humanize the space age by giving a perspective from a non-astronaut, because I think the students will look at that and say, 'This is an ordinary person. This ordinary person is contributing to history.'" As a part of her lesson plan she would have her students read journals of pioneer women and first-hand accounts from the soldiers in WWII. Seeing their school teacher onboard the Challenger would be the ultimate example of ordinary becoming extraordinary.

Of course, an experience of that magnitude was about a lot more than social history. It was about social justice, as well. McAuliffe was acutely aware that women were underrepresented, both in past and present, in space travel and as citizens, and to join the short list of women to enter space (four worldwide by 1986) was one more problem that this mission would solve.

In a video interview for her application for the NASA program, McAuliffe was asked to describe her "philosophy of living." Like most Fixers, she said she is willing to try new things (although she admits she needs a little order in her life, as well) and is very aware of team dynamics. She responded, "I've always been a person who is flexible and who has tried new things. I also feel you need a little bit of organization. I also think it's important to connect with people. I've always been involved in community affairs." Flexibility and a strong sense of team are the hallmark characteristics of a Fixer.

Like most Fixers, McAuliffe wasn't afraid to challenge the status quo or go against the grain when she deemed it necessary. For example, her classroom rules were to 1.) be yourself, 2.) do the best you can, and 3.) respect each other. One student recounted that McAuliffe was fiercely devoted to number three. He recalled, "She wouldn't stand for intolerance in the classroom and the bullies knew it." She showed this same willingness to push for what she believed in when designing her lesson plan for space. Michele Brekke, Flight Director of NASA at the time, recalled that she wasn't about to let NASA or the U.S. Government tell her how to run her classroom in space. She states, "It was very important to [McAuliffe] to write her own lesson plan. And I don't remember all the details but there was some headquarters involvement. And, you know, they had their ideas on what Christa would do, but she made it clear that she had her ideas on what she should be doing as the teacher in space in this classroom in space." Like most Fixers, McAuliffe wasn't afraid to ruffle a few feathers if it was for the betterment of her "team," comprised of her students and the students of America.

As a Fixer, her willingness to try new things, to make herself the solution to problems she saw in the world, and her devotion to her students made Christa McAuliffe one of the most beloved Fixers in space exploration.

Meg's Take:

Regulators.

Worst nightmare, or part of the dream team? If you're a Fixer like me, they are likely closer to a nightmare. Either way, you have to deal with them when you're in business (or as a human functioning within the parameters of society), and you have to do it their way.

During my time in the mining industry, there was (obviously) a heavy influence from MSHA (Mine Health and Safety Act). Allow me to give you a crash course in MSHA. In 1891, Congress finally passed a statute that established bare minimum ventilation requirements and prohibited the employment of children under twelve. It wasn't until 1947 that Congress authorized the first code of federal regulations for mine safety, which meant that finally, mines were inspected for worker safety. However, until the passing of the Coal Mine Safety and Health Act of 1969, workers never received anything close to workers' comp. By the 1970s, miners were finally compensated for "black lung"—but only for those who were totally and permanently disabled from the respiratory disease. In 1977, America would finally begin treating workers like humans, with fairness and empathy, as seen with the birth of the Mine Act and MSHA. These regulations truly protected the rights of miners, both from injury and from retaliation for exercising the right to a fair work environment.

Born out of the travesty of loose child labor laws and horrific working conditions, MSHA rules the roost when it comes to safety. They are responsible for ensuring that operators comply with every single law, regulation, and code. That's all fine and dandy, but it does require lots of—you guessed it—documentation! Much to the annoyance of miners and administration alike, mind you. Remember those arbitrary rules we mentioned that *chaos-tolerant* Types hate? MSHA is king pen of regulation, both arbitrary and critical. The thing is, it is equally important to MSHA that all rules be followed, despite whether or not the miners or I deemed them critical.

As a Fixer, when an MSHA claim was brought to my attention, I had to close my eyes and take a deep breath. It was time to saddle up for a lengthy investigation, including hundreds of hours of pulling files and thumbing through notebooks filled to the brim with detailed notes. There were countless "remember when" conversations before we could recall all the information necessary for review by the company attorney. As a Fixer, I've always struggled with tedious tasks. Alas, a problem arose and I had to fix it, so I buckled down, shut my door, and got…Organizer-y.

ORGANIZERS

Self + Order

DRIVERS

- To operate within self and order
- To create order
- To have control over detail
- To have a methodical approach
- To live in a predictable environment
- To understand the mechanics of their craft
- To use logic, reason, and analysis to understand the world

FEARS

- To have faulty information
- To be duped or misled
- To not understand something
- To have poor information
- To operate in an unregimented environment
- To be expected to work with a lot of variation

By "Organizer," we don't necessarily mean "organized," in that they always have an organized desk (although they often do) or a tidy house (although that is often the case). Instead, we mean to say that Organizers tend to categorize, assign, and classify information.

These individuals hold logic and reason above all else. It is their weapon against a chaotic world. They use data, trends, graphs, figures, and numbers to create meaning. Organizers want to understand the role or significance of each component in a system. How does it function? How does it relate to the whole? What are the mechanics behind it?

Organizers are our rarest Culture Type, comprising 17 percent of the population. They are *order-tolerant* and *self-driven*. When we refer to *self-driven* Types, we do not mean to imply they are *selfish*. Nor do we intend to suggest that they are narcissists, introverts, or anti-social weirdos (although if you self-identify as such, we support you!). Instead, we mean that they aren't very concerned with team dynamics (unless they are studying them!), and do not mind operating outside of a social structure to some degree.

This characterization may make certain professions—like engineering—come to mind. Contrary to intuition, engineers are generally *team-driven* and abhor existing outside of the team construct. As we mentioned at the beginning of the chapter, particular jobs do not always imply a particular Culture Type.

 **Preferences**

Organizers tend to gather the most information of all the Culture Types. They want an extensive amount of detailed information and empirical evidence so that they can fully understand the scope and magnitude of the project or task at hand. They continuously ask clarifying questions and strive to understand the ins and outs of every detail. Keep the anecdotal or biased evidence to yourself, please—Organizers want facts from the source.

Organizers generally master their area of expertise. Like Stabilizers, once they decide on something, they stick with it. They aren't afraid of routine—in fact, zeroing in on one specific thing is how they understand their subject matter. For the same reasons that make them experts, Organizers are incredibly reliable, detail oriented, and tend to do things by the book.

Organizers aren't particularly concerned with team dynamics. That isn't to say that Organizers aren't friendly or engaging, it just means that they prefer to work outside of a group context. They like working alone and can feel constrained in a group environment. Because they operate outside the team structure, Organizers aren't afraid to challenge groupthink and will go against the status quo if the norm is illogical or unreasonable.

Unlike Stabilizers, if a change can be explained by logic (what is the back story, why are we changing, what is the point), then Organizers can generally deal with transitions, as long as they aren't dragged out to eternity. That being said, Organizers are usually reluctant to initiate a change. Change means chaos, and they prefer order. If an Organizer does instigate a change, it will be calculated, methodical, and planned. For example, before an Organizer goes on vacation, they research hotels, restaurants, museums, beaches, and entertainment; then assigns those categories by price-point with respect to local weather patterns, popularity, and online reviews (who's got the spreadsheet?). In the opinion of Fixers and Independents, Organizers plan *ad nauseam* in the face of change.

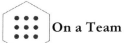 ## On a Team

Organizers, like Stabilizers, prefer to work on projects that don't involve a lot of chaos. They don't mind working on the same project for extended periods of time—actually, they prefer it. It's how they completely and fully understand the subject matter. Their work is often highly specialized and niche. They want to show up every day, knowing what is expected of them and knowing that they can solve any issue that arises within their area of expertise.

Organizers can handle solo projects. If the parameters are clear and all information is made available, they do great work outside of the group. In fact, Organizers can get burnt out when regularly working with others. Sure, they like everyone in the office, but the continuous communication (more like interruptions!) takes a lot of energy away from the task at hand. Furthermore, they are confident in knowing what they know, and don't particularly gain anything by bouncing ideas back and forth. They like their colleagues and appreciate the work that they do, but they prefer to spend most of their time working on projects independent of the group.

 As a Leader

Organizer leaders are follow-through leaders. If something needs to get done, they put a system in place to ensure that it is executed in a timely, consistent, and orderly fashion. When it comes to problem-solving, they are incredibly pragmatic. They are aware of precisely what and when something needs to happen, within their area of expertise.

These leaders tend to make decisions based on *how*, after they understand *why*. If a change is to be implemented, they will zero in on the steps to take to make it a reality. This approach decreases chaos and increases efficiency. Organizer leaders are the maestro of the quartet, creating a symphony of perfectly tuned, perfectly timed compositions. They gather every piece of information they can to make the most well-informed decision possible, and then see it through with meticulousness and clarity.

Organizer leaders aren't concerned with being unpopular or divisive. If they have enough research behind them to be confident in their resolve, they will have few reluctances about how others will process the event. They will put in place a regimented and strategic adoption plan, but they won't necessarily be concerned with how everyone feels about the change.

We see Organizer leaders operating in leadership roles that require precision, critique, and specialization. Organizer leaders can be found in industries ranging from computer science to medicine.

Areas of Struggle

Organizers hate to be in a role where for whatever reason, they don't have time to gather all the details or they aren't in a position to know what those details are. For example, in volatile industries, big decisions need to be laid out quickly, often with little information available. Organizers also struggle in a role where information is given on a "need to know" basis.

An Organizer will not work effectively if thrown assignments that are unclear, wishy-washy, or not completely hashed out. They are frustrated when leadership doesn't offer enough information to complete an assignment and they dislike actively seeking out the information necessary to get started. Organizers need detailed requirements *before* proceeding with new work.

Organizers are challenged by a team environment that demands discourse. Patiently building consensus is like pulling teeth. When they step away from the group to get a bit of room to breathe, their need for space can easily be misinterpreted by the rest of the team as disengagement, a lack of appreciation, or rudeness. If left unchecked, this can lead to division among the team.

Organizers don't typically think about how a change will impact others. The reason isn't that they don't care, but that they hold finite things, like profit and budget, over the opinions of their team members. When an Organizer makes a decision, they likely won't contemplate how it will affect the rest of the group—it's just not on their radar. Organizers' lack of perception when it comes to building consensus and gaining buy-in results in them struggling to motivate their team. They can become so focused on the production, they forget about the producers. It's not that they don't appreciate the work being done, it's more that they are consumed with other things.

Lastly, Organizer leaders struggle with big picture ideas in their infancy. They do not want to take on an idea that isn't fully developed, does not have supporting data, or has not been successfully implemented before. This becomes problematic when they are leading organizations that have to be continuously adaptive.

# Individual Profile

The principal founder of Microsoft and one of the greatest entrepreneurs in history is likely an Organizer. Like most Organizers, Bill Gates holds things like data and processes in high regard. For example, during his time managing Microsoft, Gates was known for quizzing his people about their work, with the questions becoming more and more difficult as they progressed. If someone got an answer wrong, he wasn't afraid to tell them. As one former team member recounts, "His standard M.O. is to ask harder and harder questions until you admit that you don't know, and then he can yell at you for being unprepared. Nobody was really sure what happens if you answer the hardest question he can come up with because it's never happened before." It's not that Gates is a jerk—it's that like most Organizers, he holds logic, reason, and data above all else.

Gates is a classic Organizer for his love of understanding the mechanics behind his work. in 1985, Jerry Pournelle wrote that when he watched Gates announce Microsoft Excel, "Something else impressed me. Bill Gates likes the program, not because it's going to make him a lot of money (although I'm sure it will do that), but because it's a neat hack." For many Organizers, the delight of understanding how and why something operates the way it does is rewarding in its own right. Another executive recalled that he showed Gates a game and defeated him 35 of 37 times. When they met again a month later, Gates reportedly "won or tied every game. He had studied the game until he solved it. That is a competitor." We'd argue, "That's an Organizer."

People who have worked with Gates describe him as incredibly detail oriented. As one engineer recounts, "Bill Gates was amazingly technical. He understood Variants, and COM objects, and IDispatch and why Automation is different than vtables and why this might lead to dual interfaces. He worried about date functions. He didn't meddle in software if he trusted the people who were working on it, but you couldn't bullshit him for a minute because he was a programmer. A real, actual, programmer." Because Organizers can be so focused on detail, similar to Gates, they often become masters of their areas of expertise.

Gates is a good example of how being *self-driven* doesn't mean *selfish*. The Gates family intends to only keep $30 million in the family, with $10,000 going to each of their three children. If this is true, Bill and Melinda Gates will give away about 99.96 percent of their wealth. That's a considerable contribution to world, considering as of May 2018 Gates is worth $91.5 billion.

Rachel's Take:

Earlier in my career, I found myself working at a university where my responsibility was to build out the Science, Technology, Engineering, and Mathematics (STEM) programs. When I found out that we had a hospitality degree, I dreamed up a class that would combine a little science with hospitality. I wanted to create a wine tasting class. Not only would this class be applicable, engaging, and fun (it's *wine*), but it would also be an opportunity for students from different majors to meet each other.

When I went to the Provost to chat about it, I was excited. Cue big gestures and sparkling eyes. After my spiel, I looked at him, grinning and expectant.

The Provost looked at me like I had two heads.

"How would we fund it? Who would spearhead the effort with the Board of Regents? What kind of permits would we need?" The questions went on, and on, and on. And on and on.

I was as perplexed by his reaction as he was with my suggestion. I couldn't understand why he expected me to do all that research so soon, when I didn't even know if I would get the go-ahead to do it (which was seeming less and less likely by the second).

In retrospect, I had failed to appreciate that the Provost is an Organizer. He was used to implementing ideas after all the steps were laid out before him. I don't mean to suggest that Organizers can't be creative within their realm of expertise (we depend on them to be). However, wine tasting was way outside this guy's experience—not only is it unfamiliar and non-traditional in a University setting, but I doubt he often sits down with a glass of Malbec. Perhaps the biggest problem was that I couldn't answer any of the questions he asked me (yet). A wine class was simply too risky with too many variables to be a viable option.

In this instance, I felt annoyed. However, I was only annoyed because as a Fixer, I can overlook the critical details of a project (permits) because I am so focused on the outcome (*wine*). In this way, Fixers and Organizers can make a great team. Fixers can run in screaming, "I have the best idea ever!" and then their Organizer counter-part can figure out how to get the gears turning in the machine. Organizers have an uncanny ability to break down big ideas into bite-sized pieces that can then be implemented.

If I had a DeLorean time machine, I'd present my idea a little differently. I'd show him how other universities had successfully rolled out similar projects with positive results. I'd already have a budget and a funding model. If I had planned strategically, we could have made excellent teammates and created something really neat for the students. It was a good lesson, and I knew from then on that I'd do my brainstorming beforehand, and then come to him with an already concocted plan.

INDEPENDENTS

Self + Chaos

DRIVERS

- To operate within self and chaos
- To have freedom
- To have control
- To experience authenticity
- To overturn what isn't working
- To have room to be innovative
- To challenge ideas, systems, and people

FEARS

- To be trapped
- To conform
- To be powerless
- To be ineffectual
- To be perceived as ordinary
- To be bogged down by detail
- To be in a situation where they have no control over the outcome

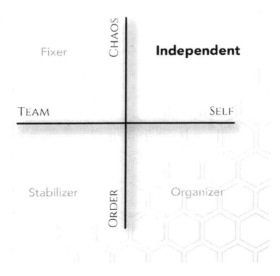

Independents orient toward *chaos* and *self*, and account for 18 percent of the population. Like Fixers, they prefer a chaotic environment, and like Organizers, they aren't particularly concerned with teams and tend to work best alone.

From the view of *order-tolerant* Types, Independents are always going against the grain, causing problems, and undermining authority. They can appear unreliable and irresponsible. In actuality, Independents just like to ask questions that challenge ideas, systems, and people. Independents live for disruption. They make upending tradition and routine a hobby. If they appear fickle, it's because they struggle in what they might describe as the confines of rigid (what *order-tolerant* Types might call traditional) structures.

When an Independent starts a company, they probably won't stick around to oversee the actual implementation—that is someone else's specialty. Independent entrepreneurs are often called "serial entrepreneurs" for that very reason. They love the phase that includes big ideas and the opportunity to create something from nothing. Instead of ushering that organization to a multi-year success, they tend to hand it off to a CEO and are off and running with the next big idea.

 **Preferences**

While everybody and anybody, when asked, would likely agree that they value autonomy, independence, and freedom, Independents crank up the volume on that sentiment. They seek agency and the power to design their world. They want to make their own decisions in their own way. They resist the old adage of "putting in your time" before having an impact. It's not that Independents are afraid of hard work—it's that they don't buy the idea that a person has to earn the right to make autonomous choices and forge their own path. For them, agency is a right, not a privilege. Furthermore, they resent the idea of their hard work contributing to someone else's gain.

Most Independents are rule benders, seeing regulations and protocol as suggestions, rather than law. They continuously assess why something is the way it is. If they decide that the *why* doesn't justify the impingement upon their freedom, they will likely throw the rule out altogether. Like Fixers, Independents find nothing more loathsome than a rule that is a rule simply because someone ordained it so.

Independents' *chaos-tolerant* nature paired with their *self-driven* mentality means that they have no problem being wildly different than the norm. We see this manifest into an ability to generate arguments (or as an Independent would say, discourse!). Independents don't argue to be difficult—on the contrary, they process data and problem-solve through scrutiny and inquiry. If they find an error in logic or disagree with a point of view, they will say so immediately for the betterment of the organization. They interpret the world by challenging the status quo. We surmise that the great mind of Albert Einstein operated as an Independent—forging his own path in life and mathematics, his genius his ability to think contrarily to those around him.

Like Fixers, Independents are resilient in the face of change. They have such a high tolerance that they can seem restless—regularly altering, tweaking, and modifying structures and things. They decide to implement changes on a whim, with what seems like little forethought as to potential consequences. When they know in their gut that they have a brilliant idea or are undeterminably right, they will hold steadfast in any hasty decision.

Independents initiate change without acknowledging social structure. While a Fixer will hesitate if they deem a change unnecessary, an Independent, much to the chagrin of Stabilizers and Organizers, might switch things up *just because they want a change*. A crucial distinction between Fixers and Independents is that Independents will start a transition not because it is vital to the organization, but because they believe that for better or worse, the result will be exciting, informative, or will offer insight into new ways of doing things.

# On a Team

Independents are rock stars at putting together the pieces of over-arching, big-picture projects. They have an incredible ability to focus on the outcome as opposed to getting hung up by incongruous or conflicting details. Their steadfast vision in the future allows them to bring a lot of energy into a project. Despite being *self-driven*, Independents can inspire a lot of excitement and enthusiasm in a team. It's not because they are concerned with how the rest of the team feels, but because their passion is so intense it's contagious.

In a team environment, Independents want a lot of control over the process. We generally see Independents either take charge of a project or disengage from it entirely. It can be tricky for Independents to self-regulate their desire for control. Without a strong iX, leadership is challenged to keep Independents engaged without steamrolling management.

# In Leadership

Independents are big-idea leaders. These leaders do a lot of hand-waving and brainstorming. They aren't concerned with whether or not a solution has worked in the past or for other companies. Instead, they are concerned with whether or not it is a smart, original, new idea. They aren't afraid to follow their gut, feeling certain that their decision will work out in the long run. And if it doesn't? They'll come up with something new.

Independent leaders generally have little insight as to how to pull off their big ideas. We don't mean that they half-ass things, more that they feel restricted by detail. These leaders, as counter-intuitive as it may sound, rely on other Types to see their ideas come to fruition. That's because when they have a new idea, they personally tackle the big-picture elements themselves. The rest of their team is generally responsible for figuring out how to actually implement their plan. Their forbearance for detail and preference for initiating ideas can be either a nightmare or an exciting approach to team initiatives, depending on the iX of the organization.

Independent leaders disdain slowly implemented changes. When they roll out a change initiative they can't understand why the rest of their team isn't already turning their idea into results. We've seen plenty of Independents become frustrated with *fast* changes, let alone slow ones.

We see Independent leaders in volatile industries that are in constant flux. They often lead organizations that are "cutting edge" or "on the cusp." These leaders created Facebook, Bitcoin, and Blockchain. Independents are found in industries from journalism to medical technology.

Areas of Struggle

Independents can easily feel constrained or micromanaged, and, as a rule, have a tough time operating in roles where they are told what to do. They want so much freedom that they can get in their own way. We've seen Independents value freedom and autonomy at the expense of financial security, emotional and physical wellbeing, and any semblance of stability. Independents might forgo a steady paycheck and a retirement plan to avoid a cubicle or put off a career for a few (or thirty) years to travel the world. This isn't necessarily a bad thing, but it can have major consequences if they choose a career path where they have to "pay their dues" or work from the bottom up.

Independents aren't known for their patience when it comes to building consensus. They hop on board with a new idea so quickly that they become frustrated when other members of the group are slow to come around. Their impatience, if not checked, can seem like arrogance or rudeness, or even disregard for the feelings of others.

Independents are the Culture Type most likely to throw a wrench into a system. Independents keep everyone on their toes. While this can be a good thing, if left unchecked, constant change can get in the way of production.

Like Fixers, Independent leaders can roll out too many changes over too short a duration. They'll run into a room with a big smile and an "I have the best idea ever!" attitude, and then they run right back out of the room. Behind them are the bewildered faces of their team members, wondering, "Is that the 7th or 8th 'best idea ever' this week?" Following an Independent can feel like trying to catch a fish with your bare hands—as soon as you think you know where they are headed, BOOM, you've lost them.

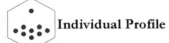 ## Individual Profile

We'd bet that Elon Musk is an Independent. All three of his companies (Tesla, Neuralink, and SpaceX) are classically independent—they are in volatile industries, they are diverse, and they thrive through constant adaptation. Each one is paving its own course in its respective field. The fact that he has three companies in three different industries suggests he is an Independent.

Let's focus on Musk and SpaceX. The mission of SpaceX is to "revolutionize space technology, with the ultimate goal of enabling people to live on other planets." Let us be clear, it isn't space exploration that makes Musk an Independent—as we've mentioned, NASA is primarily a Stabilizer organization. That last bit, the part about living on other planets, is a statement that makes SpaceX undeniably Independent. It is a claim so bold—so outrageous—that it sounds a little crazy. However, SpaceX is likely to achieve its goal. Since its birth in 2002, SpaceX is the only private company capable of returning a spacecraft from low Earth orbit and has created the first commercial spacecraft to deliver cargo to and from the International Space Station. In 2018, SpaceX began launching Falcon Heavy, the world's most powerful operational rocket.

Not only are his companies Independent, but Musk himself is Independent in his leadership style. Consider this conversation that Gwynne Shotwell, President of SpaceX (and likely a Fixer), had with Chris Anderson at a recent TED conference: "When Elon says something, you have to pause and not blurt out 'Well, that's impossible!'...You zip it, you think about it, and you find ways to get it done." Independents are notorious for laying out huge, seemingly impossible goals, drawing their team into them, and then disappearing—leaving the "how to" part to the rest of their team to sort out.

As a Fixer, it should come as no surprise that Shotwell decided her job is to turn Musk's fantasies into reality. She commented, "I've always felt like my job was to take these ideas and turn them into company goals, to make them achievable and roll the company up a steep slope." In classic Independent fashion, Musk embraces chaos by being the disruptor and relies on Shotwell to help the team get there.

Like most Independent leaders, Musk compounds Change Events. Shotwell states, "I noticed every time...people were getting comfortable, Elon would throw something out there, and all of a sudden, we're not comfortable and we're climbing that steep slope again." Independents are notorious for adding complexity and increasing scope to projects.

There is a phrase called "Elon time" which means that Musk expects things to be done yesterday. Like most Independents, Musk is impatient with his team. While that can be a blessing and a curse, it is essential in competitive industries.

Rachel's Take:

After keynoting an event, Meg and I found ourselves chatting with a few people we Typed who work for a media company. Susan was the behind-the-scenes coding specialist. We had Typed her as an Organizer. She smiled and nodded, saying "Yeah, that is me, exactly."

Her colleague, John, worked in the sales department. Like most Independents, John was skeptical of his Type and our work. He looked at us and said, "Are you sure I'm an Independent? Is there another category?"

Meg and I grinned at each other. *Leave it up to the Independent to feel constrained by a label.*

I said, "The very fact that you worry about being 'pigeon-holed' into a category tells me that you are an Independent. Look at it this way. Let's pretend I oversee a media company that has a client website that isn't performing. I'm pretty certain that there is an SEO (Search Engine Optimization) issue, and I want to delegate you and Susan to solve the problem. I might go to Susan and say, 'Susan, please review all the data since this website was launched: scan it, compile the data, and give me a report so I know what isn't working.' So, John would you be interested in doing that?"

"No way! That's bor-ring!"

"Would Susan like doing that?"

"Oh, yeah, she loves that stuff."

"So, even though you have the skills it takes to scan and compile all of that data, you wouldn't like doing it. However, what if I said to you, 'Go check out this website for me. Give me a list of ideas as to how you would fix the problem.'"

"Oh! I'd do that. Sounds like fun."

Independents love to work big-picture assignments that are more, well, independent from the team. For John, while the idea of compiling data sounded horrendous, the opportunity to work on an individualized case without strict parameters sounded enjoyable. Most Independents are easily motivated by stepping away from the team to work on a project where they have plenty of space to get creative.

This is an example of how different Culture Types approach the exact same job or problem. The language used to motivate them is different, the way in which they go about solving the problem is unique, but the outcome is the same: a correctly operating website. One of the best applications for Culture Typing is finding out what language and what types of jobs motivate different Culture Types, and using that knowledge to inspire and motivate team members.

Combination Types

It's pretty clear that Musk would land smack-dab in the center of his Culture Type. He is classically Independent. If, like Musk, you found yourself identifying closely with our description of your preferences concerning team dynamics and change, those descriptions should resonate. If so, you were plotted close to these ovals:

If you landed on these axes, you are *chaos-tolerant, self-driven, order-tolerant,* or *team-driven.* This means that it is likely you can flip between the Types on either side of the axis somewhat easily, and display traits of both Types.

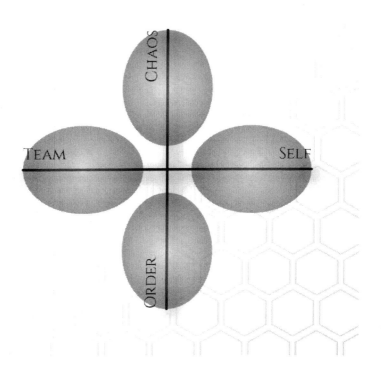

It is also possible that you felt like you possess traits from all four Culture Types. You were likely plotted close to the center of both axes, like below:

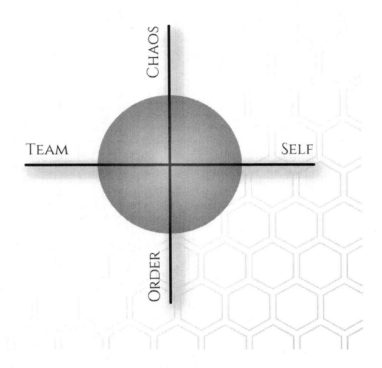

As a point of interest, we found that people in leadership roles tend to score closer to the chart represented above. Whether or not this is causation or correlation is unclear, and we aren't in a position to make a definitive statement on this trend.

What *is* clear is that leadership roles in large organizations often require traits of all four Culture Types, including the ability to work for the betterment of the team, which sometimes means making unpopular decisions. At the same time, leaders need to be able to create buy-in, and that takes a level of respect and likeability. Furthermore, some duties require chaotic problem-solving (such as solving a supply chain issue) as well as routine work, like budgeting.

While at this point we can only make observations and form tentative hypotheses, it is worth mentioning that we have found these possible interpretations:

- Having more neutral preferences makes someone more flexible, and therefore, more likely to be promoted.

- An ability to perform as each Culture Type creates increased situational awareness and thus making them more likely to be promoted.

- Leadership roles tend to be filled by an older generation, who may have learned to moderate a strong preference on either axis.

- Young people are generally not in leadership roles and tend to be more comfortable with idealism and extremes.

- By gaining more responsibility, people in leadership roles learn to be more versatile or adaptable.

- Years of communicating and compromising with all Types has resulted in leadership representing all Types.

TYPING TEAMS

From a leadership perspective, having an understanding of Culture Types gives a leader the ability to put individuals in a position that will best use their strengths. It's about getting the most out of a team by creating an environment where people have an opportunity to be challenged, engaged, and happy. It means figuring out how a team *prefers* to work, under a management style that leads to success for both the company and the people it's comprised of.

From an individual perspective, Culture Types are a tool to help judge whether or not a specific job is right from day one. The days of gut-feeling a job are over—instead a person can use the description of their Culture Type to imagine how they'll respond to day-to-day requirements.

Being cognizant of Culture Types can help leaders better understand their organization. For example, we referred to Musk as an Independent, but we also referred to SpaceX as Independent. Not only do individuals have a Culture Type, but every organization has a Culture Type as well. At the individual level, each Type can operate as another Type with intention and practice. However, they will not be able to permanently act like another Type.

A company is different in that it can change its Type entirely. For example, in the beginning, a company may need to be a *chaos-tolerant* organization—adapting, modifying, and innovating. As a company matures, it may evolve into a Stabilizer or Organizer company. A leader may choose to weight an organization to one side or the other, up or down, or make a perfect balance of all four traits. It also might mean a leader hands off a company to a different Type as it grows.

We recently worked with a large privately-held manufacturing company. It was a Stabilizer organization in industry, company, and personnel. The team was comprised of almost all Stabilizers (85 percent!). In a lot of ways, this was a good thing—being in the manufacturing industry, the company wanted to produce a quality product every single time. On an organizational level, because extreme safety and caution were necessary to operate, the company needed a "home at work" culture. This is the kind of culture that Stabilizers naturally create: individuals care deeply about one another, can function as a team, and prefer a little routine in their work life.

On the flip side, consider Tesla. Tesla is a *chaos-tolerant*, Independent organization. They have to be—innovation and creativity in a volatile, highly competitive industry is paramount to their success. However, Tesla often remarks that their biggest challenge with outside hires is that the team members who come from traditional manufacturing have a hard time adapting to their fast-paced, high chaos, "whiteboarding" environment. Considering that most manufacturing companies, like our first company, are Stabilizer organizations, it should be no surprise that individuals coming from traditional manufacturing have a hard time adapting. It's not that they can't—it's that they prefer a different work structure, tend to eschew change, and therefore need a different kind of leadership style compared to the *chaos-tolerant* individuals Tesla is known for.

In 2000, Pandora was founded by former CEO Tim Westergren with $1.5 million in venture capital. He created what he called the "music genome project" by hiring musicians to analyze songs based on certain qualities, and then having a team of engineers create software that would recognize different songs from myriad artists and genres as "similar." In a year, they had 10,000 songs documented and software that could accurately match musical similarities.

In 2001, the market crashed, and Westergren and Pandora went broke. Westergren had to figure out how to keep the company afloat, or in his words, "play financial Tetris." He barely kept his head above water, allegedly maxing out 11 credit cards and finding himself $500,000 in debt. Even worse, his employees were working for an ever-dwindling paycheck, and by the end of the year, Pandora wasn't paying its employees at all (too broke to hire an attorney, Westergren and the team had no idea they were breaking the law). By 2003, Westergren was $2 million behind in wage deferrals.

Westergren managed to keep 50 employees on board, without pay, for two entire years. Part of how Westergren did this was by having a vision that his team members truly believed in: having a democratic platform for all artists, big and small, dead or alive, to reach anyone and everyone's living room. Another essential element was spending time with his employees. He took his employees out to lunch and listened to them. He empathized with their fears and anxieties and made them feel valued. The final element? A really, really good speech. He unknowingly tailored his communication strategy to appeal to every single Culture Type:

"We all know here that what we have created is unique and it's solving a gigantic problem. No one on earth is gonna do what we've done, and when you use this product we all know how magical it is. It will find its home. Everybody on the planet loves music. There are millions of musicians who produce great music and they can't find each other. When this thing finally finds its home, it's gonna change culture. And how many times in your life do you have a chance to do that? That's what this is about."

- Tim Westergren

Westergren made this speech, in some variation, about every few weeks, when he had to inform his dedicated team that they would have to wait yet another two weeks to receive a paycheck. Westergren is the first to admit that part of the reason he was able to keep his staff is because he is an excellent communicator. He champions the ability to communicate with others as a key element in leadership and entrepreneurship. Not surprisingly, in his speech, Westergren unknowingly appealed to all four Culture Types.

To his Independents: Pandora is *unique* and something that *no one else* on earth is doing. To his Fixers: Pandora is a method by which to *solve a huge problem.* To his chaos-tolerant team members: You are in a once-in-a-lifetime *opportunity* to *change* the industry. To his Stabilizers: Pandora is something that *everyone* will love, because everyone loves music. To his Organizers: Pandora has a massive potential user base: the millions of musicians who produce great music and can't find one another.

Westergren's speech exemplifies the power of knowing the Type of individual team members. If a leader has a team with a dominant Type, they will want to tailor their communication strategy to that particular Type. If a Leader has a large organization with all Types on the team, they may want to communicate in a way that appeals to every Type. Being able to offer reassurance in the language of each

Culture Type is a huge element of retaining employees through turbulence.

ONE LONG BOAT RIDE

Remember the four adventurists on a canoe trip from the beginning of the book? Currently they are huddled around a dwindling campfire, soaking wet and running low on food. Sam twisted his ankle and needs to rest. Their trip is taking a turn for the worst, and it's time to make a decision: do they stick to their original route and keep paddling forward? Or, do they scrap their route all together and focus on making it out safely?

Independent Isabelle is always up for a change and wants to make a high-risk decision that would reroute their trip. She is concerned about the headwind and charts a potential route heading east that would put the wind at their backs, but add an extra eight miles. Organizer Olivia wants to stick to the original route. She had already charted out every ebb and flow of every river they were intending to take, and therefore it seems incredibly irresponsible to completely throw the plan out the window, even though Sam has wrenched his ankle. Stabilizer Sam is in a tough spot: his ankle is swollen and getting worse by the second, and he knows he should get back to their Subie (and ACE bandages) as quickly as possible. At the same time, he isn't keen on taking some unknown shortcut—the original route sounds like the safest bet. Furthermore, he and his friends had been planning this trip for months, and he has no intention of doing anything that would make the experience less enjoyable for everyone else. Meanwhile, Fixer Fred is struggling to find a compromise. How can he turn this stalemate into something positive, that everyone will get excited about?

Fred stands up. "West is the best compromise!"

He looks over at Sam's ankle, saying, "We'll get to town on time and there aren't any portages—you can stay in the canoe the entire time. We'll still have a great trip, and you can rest your ankle."

Fred then turns to look at Isabelle. "As far as I'm aware of, no one regularly takes this detour. It will be an adventure."

Fred addresses Olivia, "But, Olivia, we'll need you to sketch out the new route and possible places to put up camp while the rest of us pack up."

He looks around the fire. "Sound okay to everyone?" They all nod their heads in agreement, Olivia hunkers down with the map, and everyone else goes off to pack up camp.

During a disagreement like the one above, everyone is discussing the same problem but using a different language. Fred was able to get everyone onboard by considering everyone's wants and needs, and then appealing to their level of tolerance for chaos. He reminded Sam that what he proposed was only a minor change, more of a shortcut than a total reroute. He was also careful to make sure that Sam understood that the decision was made through consensus. He framed it in a light that appealed to Isabelle, telling her that they might see something new and exciting on his route. He leveraged Olivia's tendency to create order from chaos (and her ability to work independently) by asking her to plan the new route. Fred was able to communicate in the language of each Culture Type.

Imagine a C-Suite debating over how to allocate the remainder of the budget for the year. An Organizer might look at the percentage of the budget each department has used so far, and use those percentages to determine which department needs it the most. A Fixer might argue that the funds should be given out as a bonus for exceptional work that quarter or to fix a long-standing issue. An Independent might see an exciting opportunity to start a new initiative, while a Stabilizer might advise staying the course, knowing that unforeseen issues may yet arise. Each person is making a valid argument in the language of their *own* Culture Type.

A strong leader can tailor their communication style to each person's Culture Type to create more engagement and buy-in. Pretend a leader of a manufacturing company wants to launch a new sales strategy using a website platform from another industry.

To an Independent, a leader might say, "I have this idea for a new sales strategy. It's new and no one else in our industry is doing it!" To a Fixer, that leader might say, "This is a real opportunity to fix this underperforming area of our company, and industry!" An Organizer, however, would respond better to, "I've been studying the way other industries are using this new approach with a huge amount of success." A Stabilizer would want to hear, "Not only have other industries successfully used the model I'm proposing, but I also expect company buy-in to be quick and painless. It's not that different from our current system, so everyone will be able to transition quickly."

It is essential to be aware of the implications language has with respect to each Culture Type. Creating messaging that resonates with each Type offers a strategic advantage over generic messaging that might only resonate with a few people. Consider what Culture Types exist in your organization. Was there ever a time when you unsuccessfully tried to convince a Stabilizer to adopt a change with language like "new" and "groundbreaking?" Did you ever reassure an Independent that a new initiative was really just an insignificant adjustment, and wouldn't affect their day-to-day life? We'd bet they didn't go for it. If a leader takes the time to seriously consider the Culture Type make-up of their staff, C-Suite, partners, and investors, they'll be more likely to inspire buy-in at every level.

Part II
Transitions

CHANGE IS ~~HARD~~ THRILLING!

"When you're finished changing, you're finished."

Benjamin Franklin

The two most critical aspects to growing your business culture, revenue, and overall success are 1.) knowing the Culture Types of your people and 2.) getting them through the constant change that is a hallmark of business today. Now that you've got a handle on Culture Types let's talk about change and transitions.

THE BASICS

Experience suggests that change is hard. Whether we're changing our bodies, career, or lifestyle, implementing change can feel like running up an infinitely steeper slope—every time we crest the top of a hill, we find out it was really just a false summit. Even small changes, like adjusting to daylight saving time, can zap your energy (and will to live—especially if you have kids!).

Implementing something simple in an organization, like a new attendance system, is like herding cats and turtles all at the same time. One person wants more features on the new interface, while another thinks it's too complicated; technical support can't seem to fix a bug; payroll is backed up an entire month; and complaints start to pile up like dirty laundry. After a few days, leadership wonders if the new system is worth the hassle and frustration. At every turn, there is another obstacle, another problem, another reason for the team to resist the change. At this point leadership has fought so hard for something so simple they wonder what will happen when they implement something significant—although the process with the new interface has convinced them that any change will suck no matter what.

Executives spend a lot of time thinking about how to be more adaptive by embracing new initiatives only to have them fail. Sometimes, fragments of their ideas survive, but they are incomplete or half-baked. Often, they will take twice as long (or longer!) than they should have. During the lengthy rollout period, they lose some key staff. Productivity slows, morale dips, and sometimes leadership ends up shutting down the project entirely. Change initiatives are rarely realized to their full potential and seldom go without a hitch.

We've seen organizations across many industries fail to implement change (it's often said that 70 percent of changes fail to be fully implemented as planned), which led us to realize something was missing from the equation. It wasn't that the leaders weren't implementing great ideas, it wasn't that management wasn't trying to incorporate them, and it wasn't the team intentionally sabotaging the effort.

Culture Types play a major role in accepting change (which we'll dive into in the next chapter). However, there are also fundamental principles that explain why change seems difficult across the board—for team members, stakeholders, and leadership alike. Having an awareness of how we *all* move through a transition offers insight to our personal response to change and allows leadership to be empathetic to their team's reaction to change. After all, exceptional leaders don't waste time reinventing the wheel every time they want to try something new.

LEARNING TO LOVE CHAOS

Change creates chaos. Whether we intentionally change, or change is sprung upon us, once a Change Event is initiated, our current trajectory is altered and our routine is modified. Like a car swerving to miss a deer on a highway, change forces us on an alternate route. Suddenly, what was predictable, controllable, and expected is now unpredictable, uncontrollable, and unknown. In this way, change turns order into chaos. The majority of us (including *chaos-tolerant* Types) can struggle in uncontrolled environments.

International travel is essentially a huge change over a short duration, and therefore it's a great exercise in understanding how inexperience affects our tolerance for change. Think back to the first time you stepped off of the plane into a foreign country. It was chaotic! You were thrown into a world that was impenetrable; the language was a barrier, the currency an obstacle, the customs strange to your eye. The transition from the airport to the taxi lane to your hotel was an experience all on its own. You probably struggled to pay for your cab (*How much? Am I getting ripped off?*) and ended up asking the driver to point out the right bills to pay with. Once at the front desk of the hotel, you couldn't find your conformation page with your room number. Exasperated, you ended up dumping most of your possessions on the desk in search of it. As a line of people formed behind you, you wondered if this was the tone for the rest of your trip.

As your journey continued, you were at the very least awkward, if not terrified. You spent a lot of energy trying to control the chaos; looking casual, wearing the right clothes, finding a place to eat. You worked to keep your cool as you navigated your way onto unmarked buses, knowing in this part of town you couldn't pull that map out of your pocket (even though you really needed to).

If you're smart, you were hyper-aware of your surroundings. Maybe you were concerned about personal safety, analyzing the expressions of locals on the street and ensuring you were always in a well-lit space. Maybe you were trying to memorize what each coin was worth so you'd be able to pay the next taxi driver with a little more dignity. Likely, you were attempting to experience an authentic connection with the locals without looking like a jerk.

On your second night, while sitting at the hotel bar, you encountered one of those world travelers who just seems so blasé about the whole thing. She had an air about her, an *I can handle anything* vibe. Over a pisco sour, without even seeing her passport full of visas and stamps, it was obvious she sailed through customs without having to read the tiny English translations. Slung over her shoulder was one small bag, holding everything she needed for months of travel.

The next day, she offered to take you around the city. She showed you how to buy data for your smartphone at the little kiosk a few blocks from the hotel. She dodged the touristy shops and took you to lunch at a little hidden restaurant. She blended in—you felt as though you were getting a tour from a local. She couldn't speak the language, but she could say "hello," "thank-you," and "please" in the native tongue. Later, she told you that before she goes somewhere, she practices a few phrases every night.

The big difference between you and her is clearly experience. Her experience with travel gave her the tools necessary to control the chaotic environment. Sure, she didn't know what that guy on the corner was yelling at her—but she'd dealt with it before and was certain she could deal with it again. Confidence is an incredible tool for managing chaos.

Rachel's Take:

I can attest first-hand that confidence when traveling does not arise out of things going right, but out of things going wrong. When shit hits the fan, you learn something from it. After you tromp through a blizzard in Bologna, suffer through food poisoning in Tegucigalpa, or deal with a faulty transmission in a rented car in the remote forests of Belize, you are more confident the next time it happens in a different country, on a different continent. You start to realize that the same problems arise everywhere, and ultimately, that you can handle them anywhere.

That's why I've been taking my daughter on an international trip each year since she was three. Despite being raised in a small mountain town, when she grows up she will be able to handle herself in any major city. She'll catch a subway or a cab and say "thank you" in the local language. Ultimately, she'll understand that the knowing of a new place overshadows the fear of the not knowing.

Turning the panicky feeling around chaos into confidence is all about perception. It's deciding that the experience will overshadow the mishaps, and treating those mishaps as part of the journey. Don't get me wrong, there are still times when I recall a particular trip where I drop my head in my hands in embarrassment. However, I no longer recoil from those experiences because I've learned how to adapt to chaos (and even revel in the awkwardness). I can appreciate transitions because they are a signal that I'm getting closer to that pivotal moment when a strange place becomes familiar—when I remember the name of the woman at the café, when I can leave the map in the room, when I know where to find the best espresso and the best company.

In a business context, learning to adapt to chaos means learning to relax into, and actually enjoy, change. Earlier this year, I was getting acquainted with a new colleague, Steven Amiel, Chief Revenue Officer at Adler Branding & Marketing, when he asked what I do. After telling him about Culture Types and RGI's change work, I asked him what he does. After a litany of impressive accomplishments (including developing and building direct sales and channel relationships), he paused for a moment. Then he said, "The theme that connects them all is change—whether dealing with change internally, in selling new marketing capabilities, or in consulting assignments with corporations in various stages of transformative crisis." Although he wasn't surprised, he had never made the connection that everything he had ever done was connected and dependent upon adapting to change.

For those of us like Amiel who revel in change, our confidence comes from trying lots of new things and failing so many times that we know we'll handle whatever comes our way. We are certain that there isn't any obstacle that isn't a version of something we've already seen and handled. If something new does arise, we've got a toolkit of processes, skills, and techniques that we've honed through years of experience that we can bring to bear to make success much more likely.

THE FAMILIAR

"Better the devil you know than the devil you don't."

Irish Proverb

Elizabeth Purvis, friend and transformational coach, often says, "People will seek the familiar." It's why we date men like our dads; it's why we never actually move out of town; it's why we continue to drive that old Subaru, even though we know it's long past time for new wheels. We gravitate to what's comfortable for us, even when we are aware of a better option. As is so often the case, people act in business how they act in life—when faced with a change in the workplace, they will stick to the familiar even if it doesn't make sense intellectually.

Another way to think about the familiarity principle is to imagine two big magnets stuck together. If you want to pull the top magnet away from the bottom magnet it's going to take a lot of work. If you get tired and let the magnet go too soon they will snap back together.

74

It takes a lot of strength to get the top magnet far away enough from the bottom magnet before they can rest apart from each other.

This is how change works. It takes a lot of effort to familiarize a new idea. You'll spend a lot of time and effort pulling yourself away from the familiar and into the unknown. Once you familiarize yourself to change, it's tempting to rush the rest of your team through it. However, if you let go of the magnets too soon, they will snap back together and your team won't adopt the change.

This phenomenon is called the mere-exposure effect or the familiarity principle. This principle states that people develop a preference for things merely because they are familiar with them. It can be as beneficial as going for a run every morning before work or as harmless as going to the same bistro for lunch every afternoon. As with most behaviors, there are potential negative consequences as well. Even when the familiar is another unwanted cigarette or an unfulfilling relationship, it can still appear more attractive than the unknown.

The effects of the familiarity principle intensify when someone is undergoing stress. A recent study from Stanford University entitled "Pressure and Perverse Flights to Familiarity" hypothesizes, "under pressure, people often prefer what is familiar, which can seem safer than the unfamiliar. We show that such favoring of familiarity can lead to choices precisely contrary to the source of felt pressure, thus exacerbating, rather than mitigating, its negative consequences." This research expounds on existing research that suggests humans prefer the familiar, but also adds that stress increases the likelihood of choosing a familiar option. This holds true even when familiarity is established through a *negative* experience, meaning that even if the familiar will create more stress, it is still the seemingly more attractive choice.

Imagine someone on their way to work. Out of the corner of their eye, they notice a little alley way—maybe it was always blocked by a garbage truck or a few construction signs. For whatever reason, this person makes a mental note that it is likely the fastest route to work, and decides to try it tomorrow. However, the next morning they sleep through their alarm and wake up in a panic—*oh my god I'm already ten minutes late.*

They throw on some clothes, skip breakfast, and run to their car. As they careen down the streets at a ridiculous speed, they remember that strange short cut from yesterday. You'd think this person would take it, right?

Instead, as they approach the intersection, they glance at the clock again. 7:15. It's just too risky—what if it ends up being a detour? What if the other end is blocked? Instead of taking the alley way, they decide to stick to their usual route.

For most people (especially for *order-tolerant* Types), what seemed like a completely valid option yesterday, in the absence of stress, has become too risky. Ironically, a preference for the familiar is strongest when a person needs to embrace change the most. A familiar option often intuitively seems like the best choice, especially under stress, even when an unfamiliar option is objectively better. Understanding the familiarity principle helps leaders recognize why their team (and themselves) have a hard time leaving behind an old way of doing things and accepting a new one.

We see a familiarity-based resistance to change all the time when we are hired for consulting work. An organization tries to implement a change, the team becomes overwhelmed and resistant, and over time the team retains or reverts to the familiar option. When we ask individuals what they dislike about the change, we sometimes hear specific complaints (indicative of a poorly designed change initiative) such as, "It was taking too long to receive materials on the floor," or "It put too much pressure on development and created a bottleneck." More often, we hear generic explanations like, "We just didn't like it," or "It wasn't working for us." Vague complaints without context suggest there is nothing "wrong" with the change or the strategy, aside from it being unfamiliar.

A leader can't expect a change to stick simply because it's a good idea. The familiarity principle shows that just because something is the better option, doesn't mean it will be accepted or implemented. First, a leader has to make the transition feel less chaotic for most people. One way for leadership to reduce the sense of chaos is to communicate. Encourage and engage in open, transparent dialogue. Give them plenty of time to get the new idea into their space. Remember the magnets: If you get in a hurry and let go too soon, your team will snap back to what is familiar.

HABITS

"How we spend our days is, of course, how we spend our lives."

Annie Dillard

American writer

Like a rudder on a sailboat, habits steer us in the direction we want to go. They get us into a rhythm or a pattern that allows us to stop making decisions and process motivations every time we brush our teeth or make a sandwich *(the mustard goes WHERE?)*.

By design, habits are incredibly hard to change. A habit is defined as "a more or less fixed way of thinking, willing, or feeling acquired through previous repetition of a mental experience." By its very definition, a habit resists change by being subconsciously fixed and repetitive, making habits the saboteurs of change initiatives.

Imagine that, for the last six months, you've been feeling a flutter in your heart—your arrhythmia kicking in. Concerned, you schedule an appointment with your doctor. She notices the bags under your eyes and asks how much caffeine you drink. You leave her office with a simple change in mind: drink less coffee. The next day you wake up and choose a black tea with a modest amount of caffeine. It's a revelation—no more heart flutters, no more sweating, no more shaky hands. Every day that week you start your kettle and reach into the back of your cupboard, past the dark roast, for the Oolong. While stirring in some milk and honey, you think, "Just like that, I'm a tea person." Next week, you run out of tea bags, so you brew coffee *just for today*. A month later, you're back to drinking coffee again and shaking like a leaf. What gives?

Have you ever heard the widely accepted idea that it only takes 21 days to break or create a habit? The idea originated in a 1960's pop psychology book called Psycho-Cybernetics. While this self-help book has largely been forgotten, a few of its ideas have become (incorrect) common knowledge. In a 2009 study published by the European Journal of Social Psychology, scientists found that the 21-day rule is absurdly inaccurate in that habit alteration is rarely predictable, and often much lengthier. According to the study, it took from 18 to 254 days to completely break a habit! On average, it took participants 66 days.

This study supports our intuitive sense that it can be challenging to adopt a simple habit, such as drinking a glass of water after lunch or doing sit-ups before breakfast. From this study, and from experience, we can infer that to adopt a more complex habit it will take even longer. There are a lot of dieters who can attest first hand that habits aren't easily broken, and certainly not in a measly 21 days.

Creating a new habit, which is essentially working through a change or transition, is a magical combination of creating a goal, continuously prompting yourself to stay motivated to achieve that goal, and then developing habits that won't sabotage your goal. And that's when the person who has to deal with the habits makes the decision regarding the transition. It is even more complex when the change is decided on their behalf—as is so often the case at work.

FEAR OF FAILURE

"I'm not afraid of storms, for I'm learning how to sail my ship."
Louisa May Alcott
American Novelist

Contrary to popular belief, the opposite of failure is not success, the opposite of failure is stagnation. Stagnation is the death knell for modern businesses. If we want to avoid stagnation at all costs, then we must embrace failure as an obvious outcome of innovation.

Rachel's Take:

My life partner, Jared "Cappie" Capp, likes to say that "There is no failure; only lessons."

Don't you just want to punch that guy in the throat? Especially after a particularly big "lesson." Of course, there is failure. It's everywhere! It's Blockbuster and hydrogen-filled dirigibles. There are arguably more failed relationships and businesses and goals and dreams than there are successful ones. Failure is as ubiquitous as it is inevitable.

As an Independent, I know that wasn't his point. What he means is that the ability to transform the process of failure into an opportunity to learn is powerful. It's powerful because failure can be so terrifying. Failure is falling short of your goals, obligations, and desires. Failure is humiliation, loss, defeat.

Learning, in contrast, is one of the greatest pleasures in life. We love to learn new things for the pure and delicious joy of understanding something in a way that we were previously blind to. From the time we open our eyes to the time we close them, we hunger for knowledge. As in the story of the world traveler above, the joy consists of making something unknown known—to transform the foreign into the familiar.

FAMOUS FAILURES

Colonel Sanders, at 65, found himself without a restaurant or a retirement plan – nothing but a social security check, a recipe for his fried chicken, and a brand.

Elvis Presley tried out for a part with a quartet called the Songfellows. They told him he couldn't sing.

Charles Schultz (of Peanuts fame) couldn't get his drawings into his high school yearbook.

Milton Hershey had two businesses go bankrupt before the Hershey's

When the majority of us confront change, we chew on all the ways to fail, instead of on all the ways to learn. We ruminate over possible consequences; seen and unforeseen, real and imagined; and press the "repeat button" on the worst possible outcome. The trick is, most people don't even consciously think this way, they just intuitively push back from change. By the way, these same people would be horrified to be accused of behaving out of fear.

Think back to a time when you were learning something new. It could be oil painting, driving a skidsteer, or adult ballet (now *that* is a story to be told over cocktails)—whatever, as long as it was a new experience. Every time you mixed the wrong color, every time the bucket moved up instead of the skidsteer moving backward, every time you looked in that ridiculously giant mirror, it wasn't a big deal. You were learning how to do it better the next time—the awkward, weird, poorly executed next time. It takes 10-20 hours per week for *years* to excel at something. It's why teenagers are such dodgy drivers and some people's handwriting never looks like they make it past the fourth grade.

Embrace the inevitability of failure and you will set yourself up to learn from your mistakes. If you give yourself—and your team—this gift, learning will become a part of your culture. Michael Houlihan, co-founder of Barefoot Wines, believes a team can't improve without failing. He is more disappointed if a team member does not share the news and document the lessons of a failure than of the failure itself. He believes success is built on the back of mistakes.

Jeffrey W. Hayzlett, CEO of the Hayzlett Group and Chairman of the C-Suite Network, is often asked about his biggest mistake in business. He always responds, "I haven't made it, yet." His attitude is not only freeing, but particularly fearless. It enables him to embrace the unknown, rather than recoil from it. It offers the ability to continuously seek opportunity without self-imposed ramifications and limitations. It allows him to say "yes," and in doing so, redefine failure as progress. And, as it turns out, Hayzlett is an Independent. It's no wonder he thrives on freedom and self-direction. When used in this way, an Independent's drive for constant innovation and adaptation can be their greatest strength.

It's important to realize that even if a leader views failure in a positive way doesn't necessarily mean the rest of the team will. The following three tips can help exceptional leaders alleviate fear around failure.

1. Share personal failures

There is a wealth of literature that suggests when a leader shares their own mistakes they become more likable. We maintain that not only does it make a person human, but it also puts their team in the right mindset to collaborate, innovate, and get creative. When leadership reminds their team that they, too, are fallible, their team feels more confident in taking on bigger, riskier ideas. This is an especially valuable leadership option for self-driven Types, who may not intuitively understand the power of connecting through shared experiences.

2. Stay engaged

The two things we see missing from most change initiatives are enough time and communication. A leader who embraces failure is often analyzing, collaborating, and conversing with their team—they are an active part of the process. When a team member or an entire initiative fails, they engage their team and find out why it failed. They ask thoughtful questions that demonstrate that they aren't assuming their people are the cause of the problem. Did the project fail because of a design flaw? A managerial oversight? Not enough resources/research? When they get an answer, they actually listen to what's being said. If by all accounts the project should have been successful and it wasn't, it might be a Culture Type mismatch or conflict. Ask questions tailored to the Culture Types in your team:

 Stabilizer

Was the expectation, goal, or parameters made clear?
Was the entire team on board with the work?

 Organizer

Was there an issue with materials/resources?
Were the directions clear?
Did you understand the reasoning behind it?

 Fixer

What were some of the problems that you saw arising early?
Did you try to solve any of them? If so, which ones and why?
Were others receptive to the changes?

 Independent

Did you have enough freedom to create your own solution?
Was there too much structure that limited creativity?
Is there a part of the project where you feel you can make a greater contribution?

Be sure to reiterate the end game and inspire the team to work together to improve their performance. Strong leaders are quick to thank their team for their hard work and continue to engage them with the project.

3. Model failure-tolerant behavior

Make sure the team sees the risks that leadership takes, particularly the ones that don't work out. Stabilizers in particular respond to behavior that is modeled by leadership. We have a Board of Advisors, and we constantly review new ideas and asking their advice on what we might be doing wrong. We choose to be transparent to our team so that everyone knows that "failing" is a part of innovation.

Being open to new, bold ideas is inherently risky, and therefore if a company is attempting to be more innovative, they have to build acceptance of failure into their culture. If an individual or a team has an idea that doesn't work out, they haven't failed the company—on the contrary, they have gained valuable knowledge and insight about what not to do in the future. As mentioned previously, this kind of failure creates forward momentum. Charles Kettering, head of research at General Motors from 1920 to 1947, is famous for embracing failure, stating "it's not a disgrace to fail, and you must analyze each failure to find its cause…you must learn how to fail intelligently. Failing is one of the greatest arts in the world. One fails forward toward success."

IT TAKES TIME

A change event happens in an instant, but the transition a person goes through after a change event can take years. One minute, you have a job, the next you don't. One moment you're riding your bike, the next you're lying on the asphalt. It only took a second to get hit, but may take years to recover. Your life changes from one moment to the next, suddenly and often without warning, and you're left to put the pieces back together.

While the idea that it takes time to settle into change has been around for as long as human history, the idea that we shouldn't have to wait for anything is relatively new. Instant gratification has become ordinary. We have immediate access to news, social media, and communication. We can enjoy a fantastic cup of our favorite addiction in minutes, made by an espresso machine conveniently installed in our kitchen. We can buy fabulous shoes from retailers around the world, at a moment's notice, to wear to a party the next day.

What's more, when we deny someone instant gratification we seem to owe them an apology. *So sorry it took me 15 minutes to respond to your text.* We are expected to have multiple email addresses and social media accounts that are linked to phones glued to our body, so friends and employers alike can access us from anywhere.

Love it or hate it, your opinion about it is irrelevant. Whether or not you embrace our instant world, as a leader, you've been affected by it. Today's leaders don't have any choice but to stay informed, on the cusp, and up-to-date in order to remain competitive. This means that you, like the rest of us, have adjusted to a life of instant gratification. So, do we soldier on, knowing changes that take a year will just be a painfully slow, agonizing process? Of course not. The expectation that change will take time, in of itself, is useful.

Independents, are you listening?

Not only does change take time, but so does the decision to change. As previously discussed, we love the familiar. We love it so much that if we decide it no longer serves us, we can't just stuff it down the garbage disposal along with a bowl of old soup. We have to get to a critical mass, or a breaking point, in order to abandon the comfort of the familiar and embrace change. How far someone will bend before they break depends on a person's Culture Type, but they will break. An alcoholic gets kicked out of the house and stops drinking, a gambler loses her life savings and never goes back to the casino. If you think back to the biggest changes in your own life, there is one moment in particular that stands alone as the point in which you had to change. Up until then, you might have been aware your current trajectory wasn't sustainable, but needed the extra push to move in a new direction.

Making a change that will improve your life can seem difficult because you can see it happening to other people, but you can't always see it happening to yourself. It is incredibly hard to write yourself into someone else's story. You feel like you don't belong there, like you can't achieve a reality that so far hasn't been your own. It is impossible to achieve something that we don't believe exists for ourselves, or even exists at all.

Meg's Take:

All 5,655 residents of my hometown, Belle Fourche (/bel fo͞osch/), South Dakota, proudly inhabit the geographical center of the nation. That's fitting because Belle Fourche is like most small towns—it has a gravitational pull that keeps young people as close to its center as possible. When high school graduates go off to college, they pick a school that is close by (usually Black Hills State University, a whopping fifteen minutes away). Actually, I can only really remember one other student heading off to a school that was farther away and considerably more prestigious. Her name was Jenny, and she went to Creighton University, a Jesuit school in Omaha, Nebraska. In hindsight, she was my roadmap and the reason I told my neighbors (and therefore the entire town) that I was headed to Creighton in the fall. They were stunned.

"It's too far from home!"

"It's too expensive!"

"How will you see your family?"

I always responded, "It's the best business school in the Midwest, and I'm going. I'll figure out the rest." I was $30k in debt before setting foot in Nebraska and somewhat of a pioneer for my hometown. However, because Jenny had achieved this dream I knew that I could, too. Even though I never really thought about her much (I can't even recall her last name), she was a compass to a life that I otherwise wouldn't have known existed for me.

This realization led me to wonder, if my goal was to attend the very best school I could, why didn't I ever even consider going to Stanford or Yale? The answer? Change is incremental. You can only step outside of your comfort zone so far before you run out of ground to stand on. At eighteen, I had never been on a plane. I had never lived in a large city or navigated subway stations or hailed a taxi. None of my teachers ever told me that Ivy League was a possibility with any real conviction. That wasn't my life.

I received a world-class education at Creighton and have never regretted that decision. My point isn't that I didn't go to a wonderful school, my point is that I wasn't even willing to consider the possibility of going to an Ivy League university. I was limited by my imagination, which was limited by my social construct, my own self-worth, and my experience.

I've learned that powerful leaders encourage their teams to see beyond their perceptions. Having a strong iX means setting your people up to see greatness—not completeness, or the best of their abilities, but to see possibilities for themselves that they haven't yet imagined. Show them someone who has achieved something great, help them imagine themselves in that role, and then watch how quickly they rewrite their story.

On a final note, change takes time because of the pesky inner monologue we've been taught to adopt. We are taught from an early age to accept things the way they are, even if we don't agree with them. We don't like something—too bad! By the time we're old enough to realize that we don't have to compromise, we've already drunk the Kool-Aid. "That's life," swallows "work sucks," and digests the idea that "work is supposed to suck." Then we take that attitude and apply it to the rest of our lives. "Relationships are work," and "school is work," and "raising kids is work," and therefore those things aren't *supposed* to be wonderful. We watch what should be the greatest pleasures in life spoil into "good enough," and we're left asking the question, "What's left to be great?" Then when we find ourselves in a position where our job isn't satisfying or our marriage isn't healthy we think, "that's life," and carry on, keeping our heads down and never thinking to change it because we assume the alternative is just as bad, or we don't deserve to be happy, or that happy people are just "lucky." By the way, the notion that it takes luck to be happy is absurd.

Of course, just as it takes time to decide that you deserve great, it also takes time to make the changes necessary to achieve it. Success, happiness, contentment—whatever vocabulary you choose to describe your ideal world—takes time to orchestrate. That's because when the universe throws something at you, you can throw it right back. Try on a few different hats, see yourself in a few roles, and figure out what your great looks like. Because, as we mentioned earlier, if you're not failing, you're not changing.

THE KURTZ CHANGE TRANSITION MODEL

"Change is the law of life and those who look only to the past or present are certain to miss the future."

John F. Kennedy

If change is an earthquake, the Kurtz Change Transition Model (KCTM) is a seismograph. And a forecaster. And an analytical tool. What makes the KCTM so valuable is its versatility: It can be used to measure a reaction, make predictions, analyze the implementation of a change, and effect change quickly. It is a powerful way for leadership to conceptualize where their people are in a transition process, imagine what to expect next, and estimate how far they still have to come to fully adopt the change. Furthermore, the KCTM provides insight into what a leader can do to get their team through the process of change and achieve their most ambitious goals.

The idea of a change transition model isn't new. If you Google "organizational change transition" a whole boatload of examples pop up in Images. What you'll notice is every model is "U" shaped. The KCTM (based off of George Davis's model, which was originally conceived thirty years ago) is different in two significant ways. In the KCTM graph, the Let Go is a decision point, not a gradual change. Secondly, the KCTM shows an Innovation Phase, which is critical to understanding people's capacity for significant levels of change.

The KCTM measures time on the *x-axis* and what we call "energy" on the *y-axis*. Energy isn't synonymous with effort, although it is related. Energy is a metric of perception, enthusiasm, creativity, and willingness to "go the extra mile." An energized company is one with a strong iX—it has that certain indescribable quality in its atmosphere, a *je ne sais quoi*. When you step into the building you can feel the excitement in the air. Team members look forward to coming into work, are fully engaged, are willing to problem solve, and want to give more.

When considering how each Type moves through change, a few questions come to mind: "Why manage Fixer and Independent (*chaos-tolerant*) teammates through transitions at all? They'll sort it out." and "Why not simply focus on Stabilizer and Organizer (*order-tolerant*) teammates? Help them through the chaos?" It is easy to fall into the trap of assuming because *chaos-tolerant* Types tend to enjoy change, they don't need any guidance through a transition. In this Chapter, we'll explore the KCTM as a general model, and address how each Type moves through the model in the next chapter.

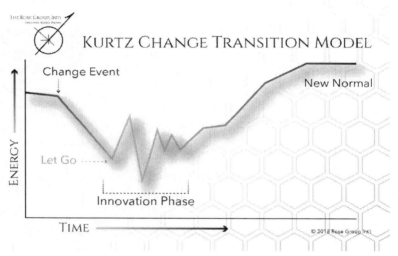

Like the rest of this book, the KCTM transcends the world of business and can shed light on our personal lives. It reveals a trend that we can use to explain why it always takes one person longer to get over a divorce, why changes seem to snowball or pile up on each other, and why some people are constantly altering their environment while others require order and peace. The KCTM brings predictability to the seemingly unpredictable world of change.

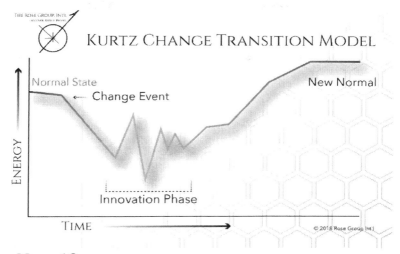

KURTZ CHANGE TRANSITION MODEL

Normal State

← Change Event

New Normal

ENERGY

Innovation Phase

TIME

© 2018 Rose Group Int'l

Normal State

A Normal State is a person's baseline. It's their day-to-day experience, or their state after they've normalized a change and before they encounter a new one. It's routine and familiar.

Every Culture Type has a Normal State. Even people who score high on our axis of chaos (freedom!) have an average, day-to-day experience. It might be a little less structured than that of someone who prefers order and stability, but it is still "normal" to them.

Change Event

A Change Event is exactly what it sounds like—a *change*. The moment someone actually moves from Nebraska to Oregon or the moment they get laid off work, they undergo a Change Event. A Change Event includes events both expected and unforeseen.

When someone chooses to implement a major change, such as ending a significant relationship or picking out a Golden Retriever puppy, they can spend about a year of their Normal State considering it. Before implementation, they are actively and passively imagining what a New Normal might look like. They weigh the pros and cons, seek outside input, and visualize themselves acting out a new role.

Consider your last major Change Event. If you chose to make the change, you likely spent a significant amount of time mulling it over before pulling the trigger. As you're now well aware of, it takes time to familiarize yourself with a new idea. We even spend time considering small changes. You might spend five entire minutes deciding whether or not you want to try a new yogurt at the grocery store. How much time have you spent reading reviews before you buy something new online, let alone move to another country, start a business, or have a baby?

Often a Change Event is unexpected. A new business partner contacts you out of the blue, your basement floods and destroys a family heirloom and the horrible purple shag carpet (Yes!), you find out your partner is being reorganized to another plant location. When a Change Event happens suddenly, it is generally more difficult to process because you haven't spent any time during your Normal State to consider the implication and outcome of the change. You are thrown into the transition process, stranded without the confidence that choice inspires.

Decline

Even during a positive Change Event, people still go through a Decline. During Decline, a person is still processing the event. Their subconscious is madly chewing away at the implications, even if, intellectually, they know what's coming next. If it is a positive Change Event, the Decline will be shorter. If it is a negative Change Event, the Decline stage can take years. The Decline can feel like you're being pushed toward an unknown, closed door. Behind that door is a different world—terrible and unfamiliar. It is a time of hesitancy.

During a Decline, people have a difficult time accepting the change. Positive or negative, for better or for worse, the Change Event feels so surreal that they can't accurately process it. For example, when people hear terrible news from their physician, they rarely remember the whole conversation. As soon as they hear a word like "cancer," they tune out almost everything else that comes after. They don't do this intentionally, but the emotional overload prevents them from taking on new information.

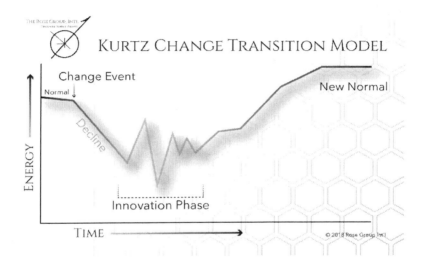

Knowing that people can't really hear or process new information during the Decline phase can be revelatory, particularly for people who often deal with the fallout of traumatic events. Consider the estate attorney, who has to walk bereaved relatives through legal intricacies after the loss of a loved one. Consider the physical therapist, who has to guide people through pain, therapy regimens, *and* a possible limited future life. The Decline phase also explains why people going through a divorce or loss of a job might seem completely irrational. They simply aren't processing data normally.

If responding to a Change Event, the Decline can be characterized by denial. People will ignore the change, withdraw, or blame someone or something else. If the Change Event was significant, they might lash out or become emotionally unstable. They may try to convince whomever has power over the situation that the change is a poor decision, and that the Normal State was fine the way it was. You'll hear hesitancy in their voice. They might say something like, "We've tried something like this before, and it didn't work out. I don't see this going differently." They might bargain, asking, "What can I do to make things go back to the way they were?" They also just might check out completely.

Individuals in Decline are unable to turn their thoughts toward the future.

Rachel's Take:

I was told one day that I was being reorganized out of a job. I understood what that meant intellectually. Emotionally, I couldn't process it. On top of the job loss, I had gone through a divorce three months prior, and I was in the middle of rebuilding a house (like tearing out everything down to the stud walls and then rebuilding). I was undergoing so many simultaneous and distinct transitions I could barely wrap my head around this fresh hell. Luckily, I had five months to sort out what I was going to do.

Instead of finding another job, I thought about it a lot, but I didn't actively pursue something else. I didn't want to procrastinate. It was the best way for me to process the multiple transitions in my life. I look back now and wonder how I managed to get from point A to point B without losing my mind. Knowing about the KCTM and how to move through transitions, I gave myself three months to process through the Decline phase, knowing that would still leave me two months to sort something out.

Let Go

The Let Go is only a moment, but a pivotal one. It's the moment your hand turns the knob of that unknown door and you step over the threshold. In some ways it is a point of no return, where you decide your previous Normal State is no longer an option. It is the potentially painful moment of acceptance. Incidentally, it is the point in a transition that inspires the most trepidation because letting go means releasing what you had been holding onto.

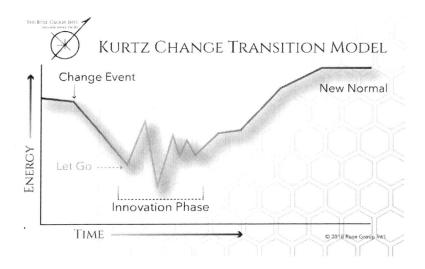

Even if you are letting go of a bad relationship or a deathtrap of an old car; even if you feel optimistic about the future and are looking forward to the change; nostalgia can still tug at your heartstrings. Remember: The familiar has an incredible power over us. The moments leading up to the Let Go are, at the very least, stressful, and at the very worst, painful.

The fast-paced, trial-and-error quality of entrepreneurship means that entrepreneurs are continuously subjected to Change Events. Entrepreneurs have to cultivate the ability to work through the

Decline phase quickly—otherwise, like cars backed up at a stoplight—changes will compound on one another, each not fully processed before another arises.

Such was the situation when founder and CEO of Xolo Outdoor, Stephanie Wiegel (Organizer-Independent), realized her first invention wasn't going to be the success she had imagined. On recounting her Decline, she said "I dumped my heart and soul into that multi-tool. It was my first invention, my first creation. I lost sleep over it. I gave it eight months of my life, only to realize it was not only expensive to produce, but appealed to a market so niche that I would probably never make a profit. I was devastated." Eventually, Wiegel Let Go of her first invention. It was something she had to give up in order to have the energy to begin working on her latest creation. If she had allowed herself to stay in Decline and resist the Let Go, she wouldn't have been able to continue the process of creating and inventing that is so essential to growth-minded entrepreneurs. Once a person chooses to Let Go, they can refocus the effort they spent denying the Change Event into envisioning a New Normal. They are flooded with repurposed energy, ready to begin assessing how the Change Event can benefit them. During this stage, leaders will notice their team opening themselves up to positive dialogue, feeling re-energized, and looking into the future.

It's important that leaders are aware of the power of the Let Go. Unless *order-tolerant* Types see others embracing the change, they simply won't move forward. Remember, Organizers love creating order from chaos, and Stabilizers are driven by team stability. So, how do we move *order-tolerant* Types forward? It's all about the 30 percent rule. If a leader inspires 30 percent of their team to get past the Let Go, the rest of the team will follow suit. Generally, Independents and Fixers get on board first, with Organizers next, and Stabilizers following.

A good strategy for gaining 30 percent buy-in is to get a small, core team together to try out the initiative on. Pull a few members from each Type and say, "I want to change the schedule. What do you think? How would your colleagues react?" Invite them to help you alter and tweak the initiative, allowing them to troubleshoot for you. Then, when you roll out the change for the rest of the organization, you already have a group that's past the Let Go and moving into an Innovation Phase.

Rachel's Take:

> *You can't motivate people.*
> I just read that today.
> Huh. Really?

Sure, leadership can't always use what motivates them to motivate someone who isn't interested. The will to work can't be infused by some strange osmosis into unsuspecting colleagues. However, I disagree wholeheartedly that leaders cannot motivate their teams.

When I was working on my PhD at Penn State, I had some friends who worked in Dr. Alan Taylor's dendrochronology (the study of tree rings and what they can tell us about the environment over time) lab. They were able to tell all kinds of things based on the study of tree rings (it's wicked cool). One August, I went out to visit my friends Alejandro and Andy as they toiled in Yosemite National Park collecting information on "coarse woody debris" and harvesting tree ring samples for studying back at the lab. They had been there for two months already, and they had their routine sorted. They had a whole crew of students there working with them.

When I rolled in, all fresh and eager to learn and work, I was a bit disappointed by the sense of drudgery that was ascribed to yet another day in the field (it's not all rainbows and butterflies, kids!). So, I went to Alejandro and Andy with a proposition. If we could get all the work done early—say by 2 p.m.—then we'd spend the rest of this very hot and dry day hanging out in the river. They agreed, and the crew was rejuvenated with fresh legs and big smiles.

And guess what? We finished the work with time to spare and hurriedly chucked off our gear. We spent the rest of the day swimming the fresh, rushing water of a mountain stream.

That is how you motivate a team. Reward them for exceptional work with something they value. I strongly suspect that whomever is dishing out the "you can't motivate people" advice has never worked with, or paid attention to, their team.

Additionally, on a day-to-day basis, leaders can create an environment in which their team is most comfortable, allowing their personal drivers to shine through. When it comes to moving people through a transition, the more aware leadership can be about their Type will help provide a context in which they can excel. Of course, leadership can certainly move a team faster and more effectively through a transition than if left to their own devices.

Innovation Phase

It is imperative to Let Go in order to enter the Innovation Phase.

The Innovation Phase is a tumultuous time when a person gathers as much information as possible to help shape a New Normal. It is when we are the most creative, spontaneous, and open to new possibilities. If you just went through a separation with a significant other, this is the stage where you buy a new apartment you can barely afford and go on a neon-light bender (it could happen, and did!) or travel the world because, well, *why not?* It's when you move to a new state, start a new job, and reinvent yourself. It's also that crazy wonderful first year of college, your first trip abroad, and the first year of a relationship.

Any time you ever think *I could really use a change,* what you really mean is that you want to enter an Innovation Phase. Artists, inventors, entrepreneurs—anyone who desires a bit of originality or imagination, will often try all sorts of new things to enter this coveted space. Monet stopped painting in the traditional style of the *Salon de*

98

Paris artists, and began innovating *en plein air* at a speed fast enough to capture the passing of time. His change to his artistic approach helped to create Impressionism and generated his most recognized pieces, such as *Bridge over a Pond of Water Lilies*. Marie Curie switched things up and used a wild new invention to study uranium—the electrometer. The result? The monumental discovery of radioactivity. Miles Davis left Duke Ellington's orchestra and forever changed the sound of jazz with his revolutionary album, *Birth of the Cool* (1957).

The Innovation Phase frees our minds from the constraints of our own perception. Like a hot air balloon rising, we become suddenly aware of a whole new landscape—more vast and complex than previously conceived, and from a perspective never before attained. Imagine from each of those high points on the model you are standing on a peak that is higher than the one before it. Suddenly you can see opportunities that were otherwise unimaginable, hidden behind the mountains of impossibility and tied to the Familiar that you have now left behind. These opportunities are the reason people learn to love change. It is easy to embrace a transition fully and dive head-first when you are aware that it will open doors for you that you didn't even know existed in the first place.

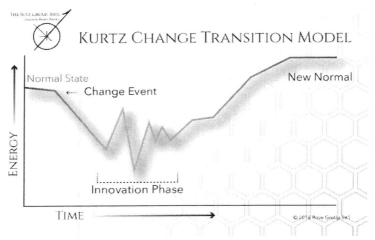

KURTZ CHANGE TRANSITION MODEL

You'll notice that the Innovation Phase isn't all peaks—there are also deep valleys. During the Innovation Phase, we fluctuate between extreme optimism and confidence to insecurity and self-doubt. We oscillate between projections of two New Normals: some better than our previous Normal State, and others far worse. The highs and lows are intense, making the Innovation Phase a time when we act as our best and worst selves, to the extreme—experimenting, dreaming, and innovating.

As a leader guiding a team through an Innovation Phase, you can see how it could be challenging. Some people feel thrilled and excited, while others have deep doubts about the future. A strong leader remains positive, inspires them to look forward, and gives them a little grace when they're in a valley.

Organizations want their people to be innovative, but they aren't sure how to do it, exactly. Ping-pong tables and beer in the fridge? Emotional safety? Big budgets? Nope. Innovation is born out of Letting Go of what was and looking forward toward many potential futures in a very real way.

The most powerful aspect of guiding a team through a transition is that leadership can intentionally create great teams. When a team travels through an Innovation Phase together, they share an experience; therefore sharing their fears, excitement, a common goal to work toward. It is the crucible in which powerful teams are formed. For some, change is stressful, or something to "gut out" and "live through." For exceptional leaders, it's a time to build and develop your team in a way that empowers them to achieve goals they never considered a possibility.

Keeping your people in the intellectually creative space of an Innovation Phase is what may serve your organization best. Your team will be willing to take on new things much easier, they will have more fun, and they will be excited to keep pushing.

In order to do so, there are essential questions that CEOs must answer, like:

100

How do I keep my team in an Innovation Phase long-term?
How do I make creativity the Familiar instead of the unknown?
What are the challenges to doing so?

During an Innovation Phase, an exceptional leader focuses on these five things to create a strong iX:

1. Keep the end game in mind.

Keeping a team focused on the end game means communicating it frequently. The Innovation Phase is chaotic, which will not be comfortable for many people. They will gain confidence if leadership continually refocuses them on the New Normal. Be sure to be on the lookout for people who seek greater control, and ask how they can help to guide others through the transition. Emphasize the way they are bringing order in some way to these chaotic situations.

2. Ensure time and space for emotional ups and downs.

The most challenging part of having a team perpetually live in an Innovation Phase is that compounding Change Events create wide swings between a positive and negative outlook. The increase in creativity leads to the generation of a lot of ideas. Some ideas will be great and other will be atrocious. On some days success seems impossible, and on other days success seems inevitable. Be ready to let these swings happen and to actively manage them if necessary. When things go awry, reiterate the expectation that failure is progress.

3. Be mindful of Culture Types during an Innovation Phase.

Furthermore, if any team members, including leadership, are struggling through multiple Change Events, set up opportunities for tasks with Type alignment. These leaders assign tasks to each Culture

Type that resonates with their particular zone of genius. Let a Fixer fix a problem, throw an Independent a solo project, allow Stabilizers to enjoy a group assignment, and let an Organizer pore over stats that no one else wants to touch.

4.   Celebrate small victories.

Residing in a constant state of change means there are rarely big milestones to look forward to. Don't be afraid to high-five in the hallway over smaller accomplishments.

5.   Be on the lookout for change fatigue.

Change fatigue tends to crop up when the change seems arbitrary, unnecessary, unaligned, or dissonant. It can also be the result of a lack of communication or a lack of involvement.

There are lots of benefits to a lengthy Innovation Phase. Sometimes a leader wants to draw out this phase long enough for Organizers and Stabilizers to enter it, too. Or, if a change initiative isn't yet fully hashed out, leadership can let Fixers and Independents stay in an Innovation Phase to help figure out what still needs modifying. While *order-tolerant* team members are still getting through Decline, *chaos-tolerant* team members can improve the initiative.

One reason a leader may want to have a short Innovation Phase is if there is little to gain from any innovation. For example, perhaps leadership has decided to switch everyone's computer from a PC to a Mac (a switch that Rachel applauds). Leadership might not want a lengthy Innovation Phase—they simply want all of their employees to transition seamlessly onto the new system.

Remember the discussion about Fixers fixing things that aren't broken? A lengthy Innovation Phase is a prime time for a Fixer to put energy into something that leadership doesn't really care about. This isn't necessarily a reason to shorten an Innovation Phase, but it is something to be mindful of.

New Normal

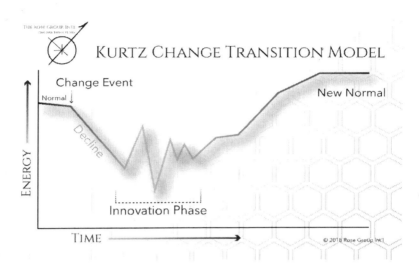

Once we have tried out a few things, explored some options, and grown together as a team, we settle into a New Normal. We have familiarized ourselves with the change, adopted it, and can now begin to operate normally again. Note: While the graph depicts the New Normal as being perceived as better than the previous Normal State, that isn't always the case. The time it takes an individual to get from the Change Event to their New Normal, as well as how they perceive their New Normal, depends on these three things working in tandem:

1. Magnitude

Did you change the color of your living room or did you change the direction of your career? Obviously, the magnitude of the Change Event makes a huge difference as to how long it will take to transition into a New Normal. While this may seem basic, as a leader implementing change, it's important to anticipate who on the team (including yourself) will undergo the most dramatic transformation.

Whether in work or personal life, if you're ever wondering why someone is struggling with a change, ask yourself what that person has to let go of to establish a New Normal. Realizing that for someone to change they have to make a sacrifice can give you insight and empathy as to why their transition seems slow.

2. Agency and Choice

Consider you or someone you know who has gone through a divorce. One person always recovers more quickly than the other, and it's almost always the person who initiated the separation. Even if the other party wasn't totally blindsided, they'll likely have a long Decline. Imagine a couple, Pat and Jamie, were recently separated.

Pat initiated the Change Event, and therefore recovered more quickly. Pat began contemplating the separation, on average, a *year* before initiating it. By the time Pat began openly communicating Jamie, Pat had twelve months to process it. That is a serious head start. Pat has likely already suffered through Decline and is ready to Let Go before Jamie even experiences the Change Event. Pat could even already be in the Innovation Phase, ready to begin dating and re-envisioning a New Normal with someone else.

As a leader, you will often be Pat: crafting, considering, and implementing Change Events before your team is aware of them. That's not a bad thing—obviously you don't want to share every potential Change Event with your entire team. However, it's important to be cognizant that it will take your team longer than you to normalize the change simply because you were aware of it before they were. It's likely you were weighing the pros and cons and envisioning a New Normal for a while before informing your team of the Change Event. Be empathetic to the fact that they are at a different stage of the transition process than you are by remembering that when we are surprised we tend to stay in the Decline longer, focusing on the past and desperately trying to revert back to a previous Normal State.

3.   Culture Type

When creating our Culture Types, we realized that the way in which each Culture Type responds to change differs. Based off of the thousands of people we have Typed and the research we've conducted, we modified KCTM to represent all four Culture Types when guided well and when left unguided. Being able to discern how each Type is handling a transition is a powerful tool to ensure cohesive, lasting change. Combining the KCTM with Culture Types is when leaders can really begin to tailor their transition process for their team, which we'll fully address in the next chapter.

RUNNING TEAM DIAGNOSTICS

iX Leaders know how to figure out where their team is on the KCTM. Often, leaders will make the assumption that their team is at the same point of the transition process as they are, but remember: Different people move through the transition process at different speeds. Therefore, it is essential to be able to diagnose where each team member is one the KCTM.

A team member in Decline can act similarly to someone in denial. They might deny the change is happening at all, or may still believe that their previous Normal State is still a viable option. If the Change Event is serious, they might abuse food, drugs, or alcohol. They might be quick to get angry or upset, and be emotionally on edge. You might notice them playing the blame-game, blaming others for the circumstance they are in.

"I don't see why we can't go back to the old way of doing things!"

"This isn't going to work. We've tried something like this before and it was a disaster…"

"Give it a month or two and everything will be back to normal."

An iX Leader never reinforces confusion or negative feelings during the Decline phase. It is essential at this point to ensure that each and every team member knows that the change is real and happening, whether they like it or not. It can seem harsh, but reinforcing denial by being wishy-washy or buying in to complaints with comments like "I know it's not perfect," will only make the transition longer and more painful. On the flip side, exceptional leaders don't downplay the transition. They acknowledge that their staff is going through a major adjustment, and are never placating. It is also possible that people will need counseling or retraining or some other support that the leader can direct them to or provide within the organization.

"Tell me more about the new schedule…"

"Who will this affect the most?"

"What will the change look like?"

"What does this mean for me?"

When a team moves past the Let Go stage, they'll engage in dialogue about the change. They may ask clarifying questions, and they'll begin to imagine what their New Normal could look like. Letting Go is essentially the moment leadership hears, "Where do I go from here?"

A leader can move their team more quickly into the Let Go phase with the help of ending rituals. Try having a barbeque or employee dinner to celebrate the Old Normal. Maybe you're sending off a retiring leader. Maybe you've been bought by another firm and are honoring the past of the old company. While it may seem silly, having an ending ritual is like putting a period on the end of a sentence. It signals that something has come to an end, and more importantly, that something new is about to begin. We recommend ending rituals for big changes, like reorganizations, new management, or mergers and acquisitions; and for small ones, like departing colleagues or completed projects.

Once in the Innovation Phase, the team will experience an uptick in energy. They'll be more eager to work, will arrive early, and will talk excitedly with their co-workers. There might be some lows, too—some people will have wide swings in mood and energy, as mentioned above.

During the Innovation Phase, leadership will want to limit options while at the same time encourage creativity. Remember how entering the Innovation Phase is like climbing a mountain and gaining a grander view? An Innovation Phase enables a team to see possibilities that were previously unknown. The reality is, not all of those possibilities are good ones.

"How can we make this better?"

"What can we alter/change?"

"Here are some ideas I've been thinking about…"

"This other branch could really benefit from this initiative…"

Furthermore, having too many alternatives becomes stressful. Therefore, like weeding the garden or throwing out that old Thigh Master, a leader should encourage their team to focus on a select few great ideas during the Innovation Phase.

Managing a team through change and transitions means mastering the art of closing the gate, or reaching points of no return. What we mean is that in order to get an initial 30 percent of your team past the Let Go, you have to make sure that everyone understands that the old way of doing things is no longer an option. In other words, close the gate on the familiar.

We encourage a "no U-turn" policy. While it's important to be open to hearing criticism from your team during a transition, it is also important that they understand that even if the change isn't perfect, it is the new order of things. Waffling stresses a team. The "no U-turn" policy demonstrates that the leader has weighed all the options and has definitively decided that the future will be better than the past.

Rachel's Take:

When I lost my job, I could technically do anything I wanted. I could get another job where I lived, I could look for work in another city/state/country, I could work remotely, I could move, I could do nonprofit work, I could do federal work, I could work for myself, I could work for others, I could get a job in higher education, and on and on. There were too many options! I love change, and it was still overwhelming. So, I limited my choices. I had a six-year-old, whose dad lived in the same town I lived in. I decided that I would stay geographically close, so that her life would be easier—at least for now. It Closed the Gate on about 75 percent of the choices and allowed me to focus my Innovation Phase in a more productive way. Through this process of continual reduction, I was able to clearly see a New Normal in the form of our company, RGI.

CULTURE TYPES & THE KCTM

"There is nothing more difficult to take in hand, more perilous to conduct, or more uncertain in its success, than to take the lead in the introduction of a new order of things."

Niccolò Machiavelli

The KCTM is a great tool for understanding how everyone moves through change at different paces. An individual's pace depends on the timing and magnitude of the Change Event, as well as whether or not it was their choice. Furthermore, each Type generally moves through the KCTM at different speeds. By understanding how each Type deals with transitions, iX Leaders can guide their people through a transition painlessly and quickly, making the KCTM a powerful tool for a leader in today's dynamic business environment.

It is critical to note the dramatic shortening of the transitions for all Types when well guided, particularly for the order-tolerant Types (Stabilizers and Organizers). Through leadership techniques, leaders can make the transition less stressful and get them to Let Go much faster.

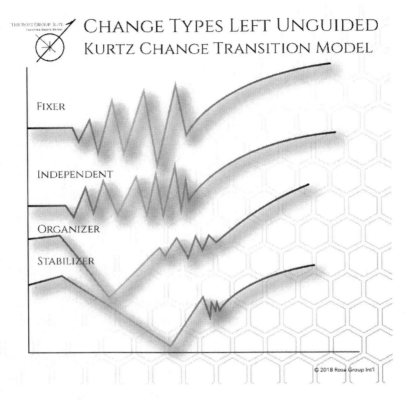

We'll circle back to this graphic again, but for now look at the difference between the four Culture Types when left unguided. The Innovation Phase is very dramatic for Fixers and Stabilizers, with the peaks and valley's rising well above and below their previous Normal State. Notice the steep Decline for Organizers and Stabilizers— without strong leadership, *order-tolerant* Types will struggle to Let Go. Finally, take a look at the Innovation Phase for Organizers and Stabilizers. Their peaks fail to rise above their previous Normal State, signaling that they have a negative perception of the Change Event. Although in this graphic we decipicted every Culture Type eventually seeing their New Normal as positive, that isn't always the case. When left unguided, anyone can percieve a Change Event as negative, especially the *order-tolerant* Types, which we'll talk about in depth later.

110

CHANGE TYPES GUIDED WELL
KURTZ CHANGE TRANSITION MODEL

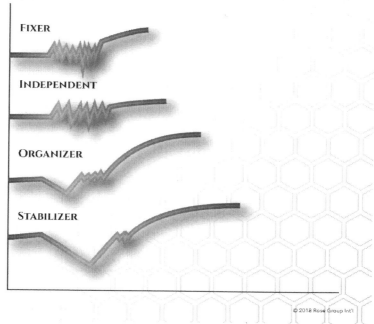

FIXER

INDEPENDENT

ORGANIZER

STABILIZER

Now compare each Culture Type when guided well, compared to left unguided. Every Culture Type adopts a New Normal substaintially faster than when left unguided. Furthermore, the peaks and valleys of the Innovation Phase are significantly less dramatic, and generally stay above the previous Normal State, signaling they are feeling positive about the Change Event.

Let's look at each Type a little more closely.

STABILIZERS

We often refer to Stabilizers as the glue of an organization, or even the foundation of the team. That is their strength: They hold everything and everyone together. As we've mentioned, Stabilizers are also the ones that tend to struggle the most during a transition. A leader can expect a Stabilizer to have the longest Decline and to generally take the longest to go through a transition. This is because Stabilizers resist change on two spectrums: 1.) they prefer order over chaos, 2.) they like team stability.

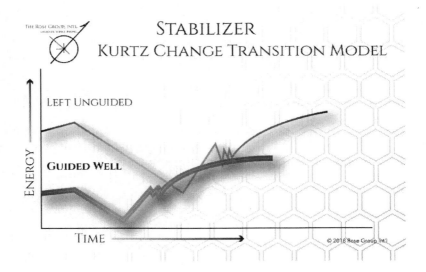

 **Left Unguided**

When a change occurs, we often hear Stabilizers say things like, "Management rolls out these changes so fast that we don't have enough time to get our heads around them before they roll out another one." Based on our research, it can take up to *two years* for Stabilizers to achieve their New Normal.

Stabilizers tend to experience a long Decline (indicated in black in the graph above). Not only is this Decline particularly long, but also deep. Without any information, guidance, or platform for discussion, Stabilizers are left in a very uncomfortable position. Their reactions to their Decline can range from a persistent need to have things "the way they used to be" or a complete refusal to accommodate the new idea, approach, or requirement.

Once an unguided Stabilizer finally lets go of their pervious Normal State, their Innovation Phase is relatively short. Stabilizers are usually quick to adjust their behavior to mirror the group, so they tend to speed through an Innovation Phase and adopt a New Normal quickly. In some cases, it can seem like Stabilizers are still holding on to the past on a Friday, and completely switch over on Monday. And once they arrive at the New Normal, they tend to anchor in it immediately.

Notice that the peaks during this phase do not rise above their previous Normal State—and their valleys fall well below it. Depicted here, their New Normal is perceived as better than their previous Normal State. That is the best-case scenario. If a transition isn't well guided, a Stabilizer's New Normal could easily fall below their previous Normal State.

 **Guided Well**

If guided through a transition properly, a Stabilizer can substantially shorten their Decline (indicated in gray in the graph above). While a Stabilizer will still take the longest to adopt a New Normal, it doesn't have to be a two-year long ordeal in which every party involved is miserable. A leader can take an active role in a Stabilizer's transition, and in doing so greatly speed up the process, reduce the depth of the Decline, and provide the means for a positive New Normal.

For a Stabilizer, a transition must be embraced by everyone—remember, they are driven by being a part of a team, and one of the worst feelings for a Stabilizer is isolation. Unless a Stabilizer is completely confident that the change will be widely accepted, they aren't going to go for it. A good strategy for increasing the odds of Stabilizer buy-in is to offer a lot of positive information up front (no surprises!). When implementing a Change Event, you can speed up the Decline by emphasizing the following:

- Provide plenty of relevant examples of how other companies or industries have successfully implemented something similar.

- Discuss the pace with them. Will the change be incremental, or will it impact them immediately?

- How long will the transition last? If it will be a long transition, be honest.

- What is the new vision?

- Demonstrate that the rest of the team is responding favorably to the change.

Like moving the foundation of a building, it will take a lot of initial effort to move a Stabilizer past Decline and through the transition, but once they adopt the New Normal they will be anchored as firmly there as they were in the old ways.

During a major transition, a leader in the U.S. Air Force provided security for a Stabilizer team that had to implement new protocols. This team was a part of an even larger group with multiple far-flung locations, and everyone was rolling out this new approach at the same time.

Leadership gave them a heads up as early as possible and kept reiterating how it was important that everyone adopted the approach at the same time. Luckily, the new protocols were based on a technology contract that took some time to complete and install, so the team had time to process the new approach. The leader also harnessed the energy of early adopters (mostly Fixers and a few Organizers, in this case) to hit the 30 percent rule. Although there was some resistance initially, three months into the new procedure everyone changed "like a light switch" from one day to the next. From complaining and gnashing of teeth, to easy acceptance and forward momentum. And once they switched, they switched for good.

A note of Caution: Stabilizers are not generally motivated by worst-case scenarios. What we mean is that they strategy of "if we don't do this we'll be in big trouble" is a terrible motivator for a Stabilizer and will only increase resistance toward the New Normal.

 ORGANIZERS

Left Unguided

An Organizer, as *order-tolerant,* will respond similarly to a Stabilizer in the face of an unmanaged or poorly managed Change Event in that they tend to suffer a rather steep Decline. While it isn't as long as that of a Stabilizer, it still can take an Organizer a long time to Let Go. An Organizer's main driver is knowing *"why?"* Organizers will have difficulty accepting a Change Event without justification. Loose, non-descriptive, general answers will not be met with much enthusiasm. For example, don't justify the change to an Organizer by saying, "We just need to shake things up," or "I'm not sure what's going to happen—it's just a good idea." These are the kind of responses that drive Organizers crazy. *Just because* is not a reason to throw undue chaos into their routine.

Once Organizers Let Go during a poorly managed Change Event, they can suffer severe peaks and valleys in the Innovation Phase. Like that of Stabilizers, it is unlikely that any peaks will rise above their pervious Normal State without proper management. An Organizer might sort out the logic for themselves and eventually normalize the change, but sometimes they won't.

We spoke with a woman named Jane who works at a large organization that recently underwent a massive reduction in force. She was kept because, like many Organizers, she consistently performed exceptional work at critical tasks. The company simply couldn't afford to lose her.

Despite the reduction happening almost a year ago, Jane is still reeling from it. Instead of feeling lucky that the organization kept her on and excited about rejuvenating the company, Jane is distrustful of the new leadership and still hasn't forgiven them for dismissing so many employees without explanation. Because she's an Organizer, she wants to understand the logic and reasoning, preferably even the numbers, that forced leadership to reorganize her co-workers.

Jane's leadership did not make any sort of effort to lead through this major, and frankly scary, transition. First, the only reason leadership offered for the reorganization of half the staff was their competition had downsized, so they needed to also. That simply isn't enough information for an Organizer (or justification). Secondly, management never addressed the loss of the employees. They failed to answer questions like, "Why was the reduction happening?" "How did they choose the people that left?" They never showed any regret for upending careers and creating uncertainty among personnel.

A few months into the transition, management told the remaining staff that their quality of work wasn't up to par. At this point Jane is expected to do the work of three people, and is now being asked why that work isn't getting done. For the first time in her career, someone has the audacity to question her work ethic.

Almost a year later, Jane has still not Let Go of the fact that the team was treated poorly because no one bothered to lead her and the remaining team through that change. Leadership never took the time to explain to her why they had to let go of half the organization or why she is now expected to do more work for the same compensation.

Jane has communicated her frustration through her upline. But her upline is helpless to explain the rationale or manage the expectations from executive leadership. At the same time, despite being incredibly qualified and hirable, Jane is hesitant to leave her job. She has difficulty initiating change, meaning that to resign and find employment elsewhere sounds worse than being treated poorly in this very chaotic environment that she has no hope of controlling.

Because Jane was mismanaged through a monumental transition, her New Normal has fallen below her previous Normal State. Jane is left with two options that sound equally unviable: stay with the company and remain miserable, or take on the risk of leaving her current employer for a new one. Either choice is bad for Jane, and both of those outcomes are bad for the company.

At the time of writing this book, Jane is planning to leave the company. She is a keystone in her team and in her department. She is considering working for herself, a fairly chaotic work environment for a deep Organizer. Knowing her preference for order, it is significant that she would rather take on entrepreneurship than to stay in an organization she's been with for 15 years.

Guided Well

Organizers aren't generally concerned with whether or not the change is going to affect the team's dynamic, but they don't want to be flung into chaos any more than a Stabilizer does. However, if a leader uses logic, numbers, and data as a motivational tool and a means to make the transition more predictable and less chaotic, an Organizer can be an early adopter.

- Offer statistics, trends, and figures that reveal the logic behind the Change Event.

- Explain why the "old way" wasn't working and how this new approach will be objectively better than the previous Normal State.

- Demonstrate how this will result in a better market position, increased customer satisfaction, etc.

- Give a detailed description of how the change will be implemented.

Similar to Stabilizers, Organizers will have a long Decline and adopt the New Normal quickly. Because they are less concerned with team stability, they will stay in the Innovation Phase longer than a Stabilizer will. They don't mind forging a new path and applying their penchant for creating order once they've decided a Change is necessary.

Charles Kettering, head of research at General Motors from 1920 to 1947, famously described people's response to change. He light-heartedly commented, "People are very open-minded about new things, as long as they're exactly like the old ones." Kettering was right about the 65 percent of the population that is *order-tolerant*.

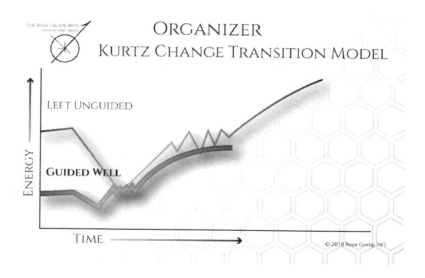

 FIXERS

Left Unguided

Even when leadership fails to manage a Change Event, Fixers will have a shorter Decline and are quicker to Let Go than the *order-tolerant* Types—it doesn't take much time for them to enter an Innovation Phase and start cranking out new ideas. It might only take 3 months instead of 18 months (remember, change takes time!). Fixers quickly busy themselves doing what they do by nature: fix. As soon as they Let Go, they are already asking themselves, *what could possibly go wrong (or is already going wrong),* and *how can I fix it?*

Without guidance, Fixers experience a wild Innovation Phase—their lows can plummet below their previous Normal State and quickly bounce well above it. Generally, their low points don't occur because they are personally struggling with a change, but because they see others around them being negatively affected by it. Remember, Fixers are acutely aware of the social landscape of the organization and will act accordingly.

Fixers are the Culture Type that is the most ready to buy into an initiative, no matter how involved management is. That's not to say there still aren't moments of panic—especially when they don't have a chance to become a part of the Change Event. That also isn't to say that they will jump into a New Normal as soon as management tells them to. While they are quick to accept any Change Event, they enjoy the Innovation Phase, and may stay there for a long time. That is their time to get creative—Fixers love change and generating new ideas. However, without any guidance from leadership, they will likely start fixing things that don't need to be fixed.

Guided Well

Under strong leadership, Fixers won't have a Decline. Fixers are optimistic about change. You will rarely hear a Fixer say, "This will never work," because they are already figuring out a way to solve the problem. If they do go through Decline, it will be so short that management likely won't even notice. They will enter an Innovation Phase with noticeably less dramatic peaks and valleys than without any sort of management direction.

Fixers are usually motivated by taking an active part in the transition process. They want to be a part of the solution. Because they enjoy working through chaos with respect to a team dynamic, they will help others move through the transition along with them. In this respect, Fixers can be great allies for implementing change. Motivate Fixers by showing them why the change is important and invite them to be a part of the process:

- Offer big-picture information and goals. Remember, Fixers aren't very concerned with detail.

- Explain why the change is important.

- Describe what they can do to help make the change less painful for others or ask for their input.

- Allow them the freedom to help modify the change.

As long as a Fixer is invited to be a part of the implementation process, they will likely move through a transition quickly. Don't bog them down too much with details or prescriptive management—they enjoy a little wiggle room in the Innovation Phase to be flexible.

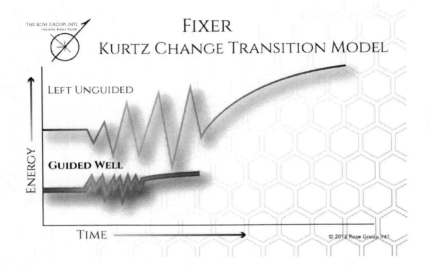

FIXER
KURTZ CHANGE TRANSITION MODEL

LEFT UNGUIDED

GUIDED WELL

ENERGY

TIME

© 2018 Rose Group Int'l

INDEPENDENTS

Left Unguided

Independents, like Fixers, have a very high tolerance for change. For *chaos-tolerant* Types, even when the Change Event wasn't their idea and they have no control over it; even when it is of a great magnitude and will affect their life dramatically; even under incompetent leadership and an unclear vision; these Types are much quicker to Let Go. You'll notice that during the worst of transitions they almost instantaneously move into an Innovation Phase.

Consider someone you suspect to be an Independent that recently went through a major Change Event. Were you surprised by how quickly they Let Go? Did they immediately start dating after a divorce, choose a completely new career path after being reorganized out of a job, or move to a new town without much planning? It is important to recognize that these people haven't found a New Normal—instead, they are in the midst of a potentially lengthy Innovation Phase.

Independents will stay in the Innovation Phase for a long time. They will tinker, alter, and adjust their potential New Normal until it suits them just right. After they normalize a change, they might begin compounding Change Events on top of one another. Without any sort of guidance their peaks and valleys have a very high magnitude— soaring above their previous Normal State and then dipping well below. They will stay in this chaotic space for a very long time if left to themselves, and like Fixers, can easily start making changes that management doesn't want made.

Similar to Stabilizers, it can take a lot of work to convince an Independent to get on board with a change initiative. Of course, the reason for the difficulty isn't that they are uncomfortable with change, but because Independents aren't easily persuaded to do something because it's popular or because "everyone else is doing it."

While they have no problem making changes when the change is their idea, they aren't as eager to get on board with someone else's plan. They are the ultimate disruptors – reveling in doing the very thing that most people shy away from or haven't even imagined, yet.

Independents aren't always quick to buy-in. More than any other Type, these teammates will challenge new ideas. It's not that they want to be difficult (well, at times they relish being the antagonist), but the thing they really resist is that feeling of *having* to do anything. Independents hate feeling like other people have control over them, even if what they are proposing seems like a good idea. The more they are told "because I said so" (which is still used surprisingly often, despite being a poor motivator across all Types), the more they will act to the contrary. Independents want to decide for themselves whether or not the initiative is a good move.

Independents can seem like they are constantly challenging leadership. They are deeply motivated by seeking the better, more authentic life and are unafraid to overturn what everyone else thinks is a great idea.

 **Guided Well**

A leader can motivate Independents to buy-in to a change by making them an integral part of the change process. Independents won't respond well to having a change thrown upon them if they have no control or agency over the event. Unless they are a part of the process, leadership won't be able to motivate them through lots of details and statistics or through team member buy-in (of course, if they are implementing their own idea, they'll likely be motivating others with that information). Instead, appeal to their need for freedom and control:

- Talk about the big picture.

- Explain why the change is exciting and new.

124

- Show how the change will benefit their goals.

- Give them a role in the transitional process where they have autonomy and control.

Remember, Independents love change—especially if the change is exciting, and even more so if it increases their freedom or autonomy. Independents love to work on their own, and can be very helpful during a transition if you allow them to have some control over the initiative.

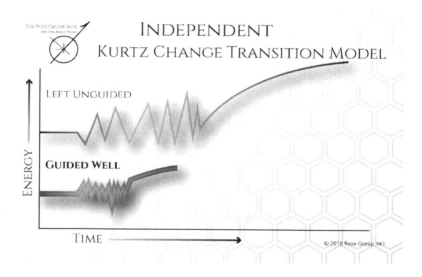

Let's compare each Culture Type again. When compared across Types, you can immediately see both the challenges and opportunities in each Culture Type. Notice that *order-tolerant* Types haven't even Let Go by the time *chaos-tolerant* Types are already innovating. They haven't even begun to see their New Normal, while *chaos-tolerant* Types are already beginning to change it. Alternatively, *chaos-tolerant* Types can still be innovating by the time well-managed *order-tolerant* Types have already adopted a New Normal. We encourage leaders to be aware of the ramifications—until adjusted to a New Normal, Stabilizers and Organizers will be under a lot of stress. This may eventually even stress out Fixers, who notice how taxing a lengthy transition is on their teammates.

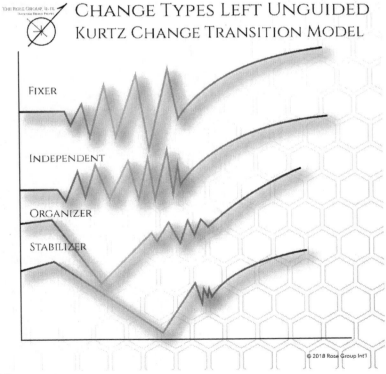

THE ROSE GROUP II-FL
Innovation Reform Forum

CHANGE TYPES LEFT UNGUIDED
KURTZ CHANGE TRANSITION MODEL

FIXER

INDEPENDENT

ORGANIZER

STABILIZER

© 2018 Rose Group Int'l

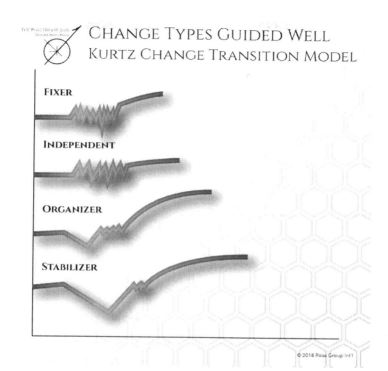

CHANGE TYPES GUIDED WELL
KURTZ CHANGE TRANSITION MODEL

FIXER

INDEPENDENT

ORGANIZER

STABILIZER

© 2018 Rose Group Int'l

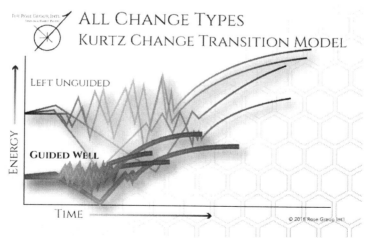

ALL CHANGE TYPES
KURTZ CHANGE TRANSITION MODEL

LEFT UNGUIDED

GUIDED WELL

ENERGY

TIME

© 2018 Rose Group Int'l

MAKING IT PERSONAL

Time and time again, whether it's a professional we're mentoring or a team member in a case study, we hear people complain about being in a funk or a rut. Sometimes clients come to us with more than just a complaint—we hear desperation. *I'm not excited to go to work anymore,* or *I feel like I can't get anything done.* Clients tell themselves a million different stories to explain it. *I'm listless, I don't mesh with my team,* or *I can't concentrate.* They think they are offering explanations for being in a funk, but really, they are listing symptoms of it. Treating one symptom won't solve the problem any better than putting a band-aid on a broken leg will.

It is well worth the effort to address being stuck in a rut. "Suffering through," and "faking it" can only last so long, and, if ignored, a funk can destroy a team.

Change is the greatest remedy for a funk. Take a critical look at your life. What is causing you the most stress? Anxiety? Frustration? Anger? Are you taking steps towards an end-goal you believe in? Maybe you picked the wrong focus to begin with—reexamine your personal goals and values. Rewrite your focus and realign your work life to meet your new criteria. You might need a monumental change, like a new profession, or something small, yet significant, like a new hobby.

At first, it can seem terrifying to move in a new direction. However, it is important to realize that to pull yourself out of a funk, you need forward momentum. The old idea that people are supposed to suffer, are supposed to be miserable at work is just another story we tell ourselves to avoid change. So often in life when we are feeling stuck we are afraid of the remedy.

When assessing what you need to change in your life, consider your Culture Type. As a Stabilizer, do you feel like an island, wanting to be a part of a team but instead working on solo projects? Sometimes you are thrown to the wolves, mistaken for a telepath who magically knows exactly what's expected without any sort of direction or parameters. When your work doesn't meet some unspoken criteria, you feel cheated. All you want is clear direction and a great team to get there with. Identify what exactly is keeping that from happening.

Are you an Organizer who is constantly getting thrown assignments without any parameters or context? Maybe you feel like a square peg being shoved into a circle, your sharp corners being smashed into a group dynamic that is both stressful and unnecessarily complicated. You don't mind working with a team, but you'd prefer to have an individual assignment within the group. Tell leadership you want individual work.

Are you an Independent struggling with the constraints of a team environment that you would operate more effectively outside of? Sure, you like your teammates, and you sometimes enjoy working on projects with them, but you wish that you had more autonomy to do your own thing. You know you'd be happier if you had more control.

Maybe you are a Fixer being micromanaged. Every time you stand up from your desk and turn around you run face first into management. You don't have any room to breathe with them standing that close. Furthermore, you want to work with the rest of the team, but there isn't any room for creativity or innovation on the project. All you want is a little more wiggle room.

Ask yourself, "Do I need more autonomy, or more structure?" and, "Do I want to work with a team or on my own?" Whether you're a leader or a team member, ensure that you are in a role that best utilizes your strengths. Nothing has more power to create a funk than feeling as though you are mismatched for your role at work.

To move through a funk, try this tactic:

Make a list.

In this list, write down specifically what is bothering you. "I'm in a bad mood" isn't helpful—but "I'm in a bad mood because of a negative interaction with my boss" is a good start. Try to get even more specific, as in "I'm feeling unappreciated after my boss didn't acknowledge the work I had done on the X project." Try to actually write down why you're feeling listless. Don't simply prattle reasons off in your head.

Describe your New Normal.

And describe it in detail. Cover the big things: Where are you working? For whom? Doing what? What is your salary? Who are your colleagues? What is your title? Then, get down to the nitty gritty: What time did you wake up in the morning? Do you work Saturdays? What are you wearing? Is there a commute?

Write down fears and address them individually.

What is currently stopping you from making the changes necessary to arrive at this New Normal? Are you afraid you will apply for a different job and won't get it? Are you worried about relocating? Do you think you'll upset your superiors? Find out what you have to Let Go of in order to initiate a Change Event. Address each and every possibly individually and with care.

Eventually, this tactic should help to push you into a transition. Remember, you won't want to Let Go until you've convinced yourself that your New Normal is worth it.

PART III
PROPEL

iX PERSPECTIVE

After you invite your friends over for dinner, you begin planning a meal. What's the theme? You don't whip up an alfredo sauce to pour over steaks and your friends don't think you're making Thai when they can smell Italian. You can have a great recipe for scrumptious duck *confit* and follow it to a "t" but if you don't know how it's supposed to taste, you'll never really know if you've got it right.

In the same way, we can't, in good conscience, hand over the recipe for iX Leadership without explaining the essence of the thing: the feeling of the idea, the philosophy that we find so integral to success that we not only live by it personally but also share it with the world.

So, we won't.

What does it mean to be an iX Leader, Company, or Human? What philosophies and beliefs will roll around in your head until you think in the language of iX? How can you enter the mindset that will really allow you to take advantage of Culture Types and the KCTM?

Meg's Take:

When I was a kid, I had a great volleyball coach. While she had us run drill after drill and play after play until we'd mastered it, there was something more to her style than her tactical approach. She had a way of helping each player get into a forward-thinking headspace. She would say things like, "What happened in the last five seconds isn't going to change, improve or ruin what happens in the next five, so forget about it and get moving!" She challenged us to let go of the past and look toward the future.

The iX Perspective starts with framing your perception. It's about letting go of what *was* and focusing on what *will be*. To keep our minds focused on what we can achieve, rather than what we can't, we created a process called "Burn the Bad, Keep the Good." This tool peels away negative feelings and thoughts. Whether they are your own thoughts or imposed on you by others, you have to let them go.

Take 15 minutes and do this exercise, seriously, right now. It'll be the best 15 minutes you've ever spent. Get a postcard-sized piece of paper and write down every doubt you have about yourself: your shortcomings, your success, your career, your organization, your department. Tease out the things you've stuffed deep in the back of your mind, like "I'm fat, I'm not good enough, I don't deserve it, I'm a disappointment." Accept who you are. Stop believing other people's perceptions of you, like, "You're too short, too female, too gay, too young, too old." All of it: Write it down! Write it down even if you think you've dealt with it already. Write it down even if you've paid a great counselor lots of money to do it for you.

Once you've written them down, take another postcard-sized piece of paper and write down three to five things you will have in your life in the next year. Yes, I said, "You *will* have." Don't write down what you want, desire, or hope for—write it as if there is a 100 percent chance it *will* happen. Now, grab that list of doubts and add to it if you need to. Look it over—really look it over—because this is the last time you get to think those thoughts, you're going to let them go. Completely, forever.

Fold up the list of doubts and find a safe place to light it on fire. Burn the Bad! Get rid of those doubts! They weren't serving you in the first place and are no longer something to make excuses with. Grab that list of good, look it over and get used to always thinking you will reach those goals, the next goals, all goals because this is your New Normal.

Now, in order to make sure all of that sticks, you have to know a few more things. We have to talk about Living in Choice. You get to decide every day how your life will go. From deciding how many times a day to brush your teeth to picking a life partner, a career, and a car, you decide. You can let people, situations, and timing get to you but who does that serve? If you choose every day to be positive, purposeful, and driven you have a much higher chance of keeping the bullshit from getting into your head.

Begin to familiarize yourself with the stories, a.k.a. excuses, you tell yourself. How easy are you making it for yourself to not be better, get what you want, succeed? How are you getting in your own way? Henry Ford is credited with coining the phrase, "Whether you think you can or whether you think you can't, you're right." The reality is when we make excuses we build our own roadblocks. Becoming familiar with how you personally deal with these "stories" gives you a leg up on mastering the iX Perspective.

The last important piece of the iX Perspective is the folks you surround yourself with. Rachel always says, "If you're in a room with five millionaires, you're the sixth. If you're in a room with five smokers, you're the sixth." Which room do you want to be in? Who do you want to be defined by? How do you want to be held accountable? Find those people and don't let them go.

It's imperative that you understand these concepts, but more importantly, they need to become a part of your psyche. The iX Perspective is casting off doubt, believing 100 percent in your success, and letting go of those damned stories. Humble up, live in choice, share your vision, and help your team. Live iX.

This isn't the first leadership book to discuss Values, Vision, Accountability, and Empathy, and it won't be the last. The business world has been talking about Values, Vision, and Accountability since John P. Kotter's *Leading Change* (1996), and we've been debating Empathy in leadership for the past five years. However, with a working knowledge of Culture Types and the KCTM, you now have a better way to approach classic leadership. Part of becoming an iX Leader is being able to craft a Vision that resonates with your people. It's knowing *when* and *what* to hold your team accountable to. An iX Leader empathizes with their team for the right reasons, in the right situations.

VALUES

In 1994, Hamdi Ulukaya immigrated to New York City with a few
thousand dollars in his pocket. As a Kurd, Ulukaya had fled prejudice
in Turkey and arrived as an anti-capitalist in the hallmark of
capitalism. Whatever his feelings toward America, it was his only
logical alternative to oppression. In broken English, he managed to
take a cab to Long Island's Adelphi University, where he would study
English and come to appreciate American culture in the process.

When his father came to visit in 1996, Ulukaya set out to stock
his refrigerator with breakfast foods his father was familiar with
(Captain Crunch wasn't an option). While it was easy enough to find
decent bread and olives, Ulukaya failed to find any feta cheese that
was up to par with his Kurdish palate. While lamenting over the
bland, watery cheese Ulukaya bought from the store, his father
pointed out that it likely wasn't that Americans wouldn't enjoy good
feta, but that they didn't have the opportunity to try it. He suggested
Ulukaya create a Kurdish feta on American soil.

Coming from a family of goat farmers, Ulukaya didn't anticipate
his life's work becoming a version of what his parents did in
Turkey—repackaging the family business and selling it to a different
continent wasn't exactly his dream. However, as he spent more time
mulling it over, he realized his father was right in seeing an
opportunity for Greek foods in the market. After two years of
making Euphrates feta cheese, he began to turn a profit. When Kraft
closed a yogurt and cheese factory, he jumped on the opportunity to

expand into the yogurt market. With the purchase of the factory, Ulukaya was realizing his vision.

Ulukaya loved Greek yogurt as a child, and thought more Americans would too, if only they could find a reasonably priced option with a name they could pronounce at their local super market. Similar to the shortage of tasty feta, Ulukaya figured Americans simply didn't have a good yogurt option. At the time, Fage yogurt (pretty much the only Greek-style yogurt on the shelves at the time) held a measly one percent of the yogurt industry. The rest of the industry was dominated by overly sweetened and preservative-laden yogurts of artificial pinks, unnatural blues, and strange yellows. The shelves of the American supermarket were ripe with opportunity, and the American palate was hungry for something new.

Ulukaya and Chobani reached $1 billion in revenue in just five years. Since then, the Greek yogurt industry has exploded to a $3.6 billion industry, with Chobani dominating the market. As of June 2018, Ulukaya's net worth is $1.7 billion. We'd bet his view of capitalism has changed over the years. Rebecca Mead, author and contributor to *The New Yorker*, points out that Ulukaya's vision was realized in the same spirit this country is built on: "With Chobani, Ulukaya has transformed a product with a distinctly ethnic identity into an entirely American product—and this kind of transformation is the most American story there is."

Ulukaya saw his success as a platform to showcase his values. He strives to employ immigrants and has made generous contributions to humanitarian efforts. He has adopted a six-week parental-leave policy and has launched a program that will give up to 10 percent of Chobani's equity to his workers. As a sponsor of the London Olympics, Ulukaya took his first five employees to watch the games, for free. When he asked his employees to work over Christmas day, he gave everyone a prime rib feast. Every Thanksgiving, he gives his employees a turkey and a bucket of feta cheese. After a product recall, he donated $1.5 million to Cornell's food-science department to fund research into food safety and training protocols for dairy workers.

Whatever your values may be, as a leader you are in a unique position to uphold them. Like Ulukaya, you get to choose how you respond to adversity and criticism, as well as how you treat your customers, stakeholders, and team members. It's important to recognize what you care about, and in turn do what it takes to ensure your company mirrors your values.

ASPIRATIONAL GOALS

"Name your goal. Tell the universe. Get started."

Meg Manke

Aspirational goals create beauty, inspire creativity, and invite meaning. It's why Charles Babbage began working on the first computer, the Analytical Engine. It's why Henry Ford helped to turn a carriage into a car for the masses, and why Thomas Edison gave us light. It's why we've left footprints on the moon and why Elon seems to be single-handedly rewriting our story about how we're going to someday inhabit other planets.

The first sign of having an aspirational goal is most people think you're crazy. You might even think you're crazy (in our experience you definitely do). The beauty of an aspirational goal is that it's something that you have to squint your eyes to just barely make out on the horizon. It's there, within your grasp, but it's going to take a really long reach to get it.

Courtney Dauwalter was reaching for something when she signed up for the Moab 240— a massive solo, non-stop endurance footrace. The 238.3-mile loop (yes, you read that correctly) boasts a total elevation change of 58,934 feet (17,964 meters). That's almost one thousand more feet of elevation change than that of Mount Everest.

The race begins in the small desert town of Moab, Utah, and winds its way over mesas and slickrock and through steep canyons and gorges. After running 100 miles south to the dry Abajo Mountains, runners head north again, through the hot desert afternoon and cold desert night (the lowest temperature was 9 degrees during the race). At mile 149, runners find themselves climbing up and over the epic La Sal Mountains at 10,000 feet elevation. From the foothills of the mountains, they stagger back into Moab after running just 30 miles shy of what it would take to run the entire width of Utah. The cut-off time in 2017 was set at 112 hours, or almost *five* days.

Courtney Dauwalter won the Moab 240 race outright in 2 days, 9 hours, and 55 minutes. She beat second-place Sean Nakamura by more than 10 hours. She managed to average 14.6-minute miles and 97.7 miles per day over terrain some of us are nervous to walk on. She slept twice during the race, totaling 21 minutes of rest. One of her naps was a mere minute, which she took after nearly falling asleep while running. She ran through debilitating physical pain, mental walls, dehydration, delirium, and even hallucinations. During a prior race, called Run Rabbit Run 100, she finished the last twelve miles totally blind from a corneal edema and a concussion.

During an interview with Joe Rogan, Rogan asked Dauwalter how she continues to set record times through intense physical pain and mental fatigue. He assumed part of her success had to be in some sort of crazy training regimen paired with a strict diet. On the contrary, Dauwalter says she ran 100 miles a week on average to prepare for the race, which was relatively low compared to competitors like Cameron Hanes, who was running a marathon a day. She said her diet is very American: beer, nachos and a multi-vitamin. While she attributed some of her physical success to living at a high altitude, she suggests its really her tenacity that pulled her through.

She mused, "I don't know that I'm physically better than any of [my competition] ...I keep doing these races that put me in uncomfortable physical states, and then I try and keep in mind my brain can help me overcome this physical pain. In this past couple years, it has been not letting myself have an excuse to stop [running]."

Dauwalter set an aspirational goal: to complete the Moab 240. Then she ran. She knew that there wasn't a magic potion—like a fad diet or weird workout—that would suddenly make her faster and stronger. The answer to achieving her aspiration and transcending the physical barriers of her body was simple: Just keep running. Run through heat, through dehydration; run down steep gorges and up mountain passes; run despite aching muscles, despite exhaustion, despite delirium.

The answer to anyone's aspirational goal can be just as simple: Keep working. Hamdi Ulukaya said that the two years he toiled in his cheese factory in order to gain enough capital to buy Chobani's first yogurt factory were some of the most arduous days of his entire life. He'd often sleep on the road, working to make deliveries on time. He spent most days covered in whey from the factory. He struggled to find good employees, fund the factory, and establish wholesale buyers. It takes work to realize your vision, and as Thomas Edison famously said, "Opportunity is missed by most people because it is dressed in overalls and looks like work." We couldn't agree more.

SETTING YOUR STANDARDS

Ulukaya and Dauwalter couldn't have achieved their level of success without creating a strong set of values. Values are a compass rose. They direct you to your desired outcome by orienting your daily routine to your big picture. They are particularly useful when you veer off course and are struggling to make sense of what comes next.

140

When you lose a big client, have a discouraging shareholder meeting, or fail to meet your sales target, your compass rose will realign your strategy and set you moving in the right direction again.

The process of creating a values system is a lot more courageous and involved than just picking something that sounds good. The most difficult aspect can be knowing what you *actually* want. Often, we think things like, *I want to be a millionaire,* or *I want to help people.* The problem with loose, non-specific values is that they don't answer *why* and they definitely don't answer *how.* To answer those questions, identify the need for your company (why you are valuable), your passion, and your core values, which together will give you a vision.

For example, RGI's mission statement was created out of the following items:

Need

We invented our Culture Types because we saw a gap in our industry. At the time, current personality profiles weren't translating into results for organizations. We created something that does.

Passion

We're passionate about strong project management and talent management. We love interacting with people and making a meaningful impact in their work life.

Core Values

We believe in providing value, leveraging energy, philanthropy, and fun.

Our passion and core values together created RGI, whose vision is to revolutionize the way leaders view and leverage the energy of their people.

Making a values system clear, concise, and known will make a company flexible. Using a set of values as a lens to view new opportunities through can be helpful for both order-tolerant and chaos-tolerant Types. It offers Stabilizers and Organizers a system to help assess any surprises, and therefore helps to make order out of chaos. Having an evaluation method already in place when opportunity arises streamlines the process of deciding whether a project, client, etc., will take an organization in the right direction. For *chaos-tolerant* Types, a values system keeps them focused and goal-oriented.

VISION

"The important achievement of Apollo was demonstrating that humanity is not forever chained to this planet and our visions go rather further than that and our opportunities are unlimited."

Neil Armstrong
Astronaut and First Human on the Moon

Creating a vision and seeing it through starts with the all-powerful list. Identify long-term goals. The more specific, the better. *I will increase sales 5 percent by December 1 of 2025* is much more powerful than *I will increase sales*. Jim Carrey is famous for this kind of mindset work. According to an interview he had on *The Oprah Winfrey Show*, in 1985 he was a struggling comedian and flat broke. He'd drive up to Mulholland drive and visualize directors and people he admired telling him, "I like your work." He'd remind himself that his goals were achievable: "They exist, I just don't have them—yet." One of those nights, he wrote himself a check for 10 million dollars for "acting services rendered," and dated it thanksgiving of 1995. He kept it in his wallet. Just before 1995, he found out he was going to make 10 million dollars for *Dumb and Dumber*. Looking back on the interview, Oprah mused, "If you can see it and believe it, it's a lot easier to achieve it."

Carrey made another interesting point in that interview. He argued that visualization is accomplished through cultivating strong values, then adopting habits to ensure you reach it. Or, in his words, "You can't visualize and then go eat a sandwich." What he means is you can't simply create a vision and then wait for it to come to you. You have to set yourself up for success. Write down a ten-year goal, a five-year goal, a one-year goal, monthly goals, and daily goals. Ask at the beginning of each day what you are going to do *that day* to make your vision achievable.

Meg's Take:

I was five years old when I learned the concept behind "vision." My dad and I were riding our horses through one of our 500-acre pastures of grassland. I was perched on top of Ginger, my first horse. On that morning we weren't out riding for fun—we needed to herd cows into a nearby pasture, and I was finally old enough to help. My dad looked over at me as he leaned his arms against his saddle horn.

"All right Meg, just remember, if you get lost stay calm and find a fence. No matter how far away you get, you keep following that fence in any direction and you'll make it back to the barn. Okay?"

"Okay I got it. Ging' and I can handle it," I replied. I had been in this pasture so many times with him that I was confident I knew where I was going. I looked up at him, smiling.

He nodded toward the south and said, "You head toward those hills over there. I'll head along the draw to the north. In about thirty minutes, we'll meet in the middle and ride back to the barn together with the cows."

"Got it!" I yelled over my shoulder. I barely heard him—Ginger and I were already at a trot, determined to prove to dad that we were up to the task.

Everyone thinks South Dakota is completely flat. That's mostly true, but the land does roll a little bit. You can't always tell because the grass is uniform in color and texture—one block of swaying green. Sometimes the only way to see hills and valleys is to focus on something on the horizon and wait until it dips into a draw. Suddenly, it disappears.

After ten minutes of riding I looked over my shoulder, and dad was gone. Just like that, Ginger and I were totally alone. For *miles*. We put on the brave face of a stubborn kid and her horse and rounded up the cows. My heart raced as we made our way to the west end of

144

the pasture, where I thought dad and I were going to meet. He wasn't there.

When you're a kid, time doesn't really act like it should. What was twenty minutes seemed like hours. My eyes widened with post-apocalyptic, doomsday fear. *Where is he? Did he forget about me? Where is the barn? OH MY GOD, THE END OF TIMES I'M GOING TO DIE OUT HERE ALONE!*

I looked down at Ginger, hoping she might know how to get back to the barn. She shook her mane, "No." Sobbing, I managed to remember what dad had said before I left: "Stay calm and find a fence." I took a few deep breaths and looked around. I didn't recognize my surroundings, but there was a fence twenty yards away. I rounded up the cows and pointed Ginger toward it.

We followed that fence for thirty minutes as I struggled to keep the cows together. By the time we got to the barn, dad was waiting for us. I was still crying, and he looked anxious. He gave me a big hug and asked,

"What the hell happened?!"

"I couldn't find you, so I found a fence."

I didn't meet my dad where I was supposed to, but on a larger scale, that wasn't my dad's vision. The goal was to move the cows to the barn. Even though I didn't do my job the way Dad intended, he had given me all the tools I needed to finish the job any way I could. I got lost, so I found a fence.

As a leader, having a unified vision means making a plan and ensuring everyone knows how to get there. People might choose different paths, but that ultimately doesn't matter as long as strong lines of communication are in place so that everyone ends at the same destination, at roughly the same time. Not only does it not matter, but it can be a strategy. As long as a leader keeps in mind everyone's Culture Type, allowing a team to forge a new path can inspire innovative thinking and creativity. A unified vision creates intellectual cohesion by bringing all sets of genius to the table and sets them spinning in the same direction.

One of the many nuances of leadership is realizing how to manifest your own vision as well as your team's vision. That requires time to think about how to leverage the talent of each person to ensure they can perform optimally within their role. When creating or changing a team, get to know you're the individual values of your teammates. What do they like? What do they hate? What kinds of projects and tasks do they have a propensity to finish? Ask yourself how you can accommodate them. Making people do things they don't want to do isn't strong leadership and will seriously impede productivity.

Leaders can't make everyone happy, and we aren't proposing that be the goal. However, productivity is the goal, and employee engagement is instrumental to productivity. Just because leadership can't put their people in positions they will enjoy *every single time* doesn't mean leadership shouldn't strive to make their people's work life more meaningful. We hear ineffectual leaders make comments like, "They're at work, they aren't supposed to be happy," or "I'm not paying them to be happy." These statements aren't justification, they're excuses that alleviate leadership of the necessary effort it takes to ensure each member of the team is performing a task that they enjoy, and are therefore performing at an optimal level.

Cy Wakeman, psychologist and founder of Reality Based Leadership, is a proponent of this leadership strategy. When a leader asks her advice on what to do with a problem employee, her response is to disengage with that employee: "I have one staff member who totally runs the show, and controls everything. Since I came into a managing position above them, I'm trying to change things but it's hard because they won't cooperate." Her answer? "Work with the willing," and "Buy-in is a choice." We agree that buy-in is a choice, but we strongly disagree that leadership is excused from earning it. If leadership isn't willing to work with their staff, why would they be willing to work with leadership? Furthermore, blaming the employee for lack of buy-in **doesn't solve the problem**. With employee disengagement at 68 percent (Gallup), a leader would have to fire almost 2/3 of their workforce in order to actually implement Wakeman's approach to only "work with the willing." At that rate, who is left to work with?

We're always surprised by this approach to leadership. When the vision of the company and the team align, the team is far more productive. As a leader, ask your teammates what part of their job they enjoy and what types of work they excel at. Pair that knowledge with their Culture Type, and you will have a tailored approach to a truly unstoppable team with razor-sharp focus.

For example, if a leader has Independents on their team, they really need to sell the project up front to get them on board with the company vision. They aren't going to take leadership's excitement at face-value. Independents need to hear what makes the project new, creative, or exciting. How is it different from other projects you've done before? What will it accomplish? Remember, Independents thrive on the big-picture. They aren't particularly interested in *how* but are interested in *why*. If possible, give them part of the project that they can manage on their own terms, with a vision that they can modify and rework themselves.

Fixers tend to focus on problems in the project. The moment leadership lays out the plan, they are playing out potential setbacks in their head. They are masters of *what if* and contingency plans. Ask yourself if there are areas of the project that aren't totally hashed out. If that's the case, let your Fixers tackle it. Sara Blakely, the billionaire who invented leggings, says, "If somebody can do something 80 percent as good as you think you would have done it yourself, then you've got to let it go." We might modify that sentiment to say, "If you have a problem that you don't have time to solve, give it to a Fixer. They might fix it better than you would."

Stabilizers are the mortar that hold teams together. They are the great unifiers—and therefore, while some Culture Types are better suited for different jobs, almost every team needs Stabilizers. A Stabilizer will see the project through to its very end, as long as leadership doesn't pressure them to be in the spot light or assign them solo projects without support from leadership and the team. While Independents are inspired by *why*, Stabilizers are inspired by how. Give them vision through clarity: They thrive with strict parameters, clear goals, and straightforward language. Like an Organizer, don't make a Stabilizer figure out what their role is. That's *your* job. Stabilizers enjoy knowing what everyone's role is so that they know exactly where they fit within the structure of the team.

Organizers want the data. Keep your opinion and your sales pitch to yourself—these teammates want to see the numbers and decide for themselves. While a Fixer or Independent might be motivated by an avant-garde, surprising idea, Organizers want to see data that suggests the project will work. If the project doesn't necessarily have raw data to show, make a case using practical, critical thinking as your basis. Align Organizers' focus by sharing trends, studies, projections, etc., and then give them a very specific job. Organizers don't like guesswork, and will lose focus on the bottom line if they are constantly trying to decode what the leader expects of them.

During a case study, RGI realized an Organizer was jeopardizing the team because he thought he was doing a process correctly and that the rest of the team was mistaken, which put him infinitely at odds with the rest of his team. Furthermore, *he* was the one who was mistaken. We knew that he wasn't a bad team member, but we also knew that in order to align him with the vision of the rest of the team and the organization, we had to show him the data to get him on board. We had to prove, through logic and numbers, that in fact, the team was on the right track and he was misinterpreting the data. Once he understood the process, he immediately changed his tune.

148

He transformed from an antagonist into a team player. In that way, we realigned his focus with that of the organization. More importantly, we did so without devaluing or alienating him, and therefore avoided creating an even *bigger* problem.

ORGANIZATIONAL VISION

Organizational vision is usually the most difficult to align with individual vision because it is the furthest removed from the experience of the employee. The challenge is aligning revenue, cost reduction, shareholder influence, and other C-Suite values with the myriad individual values on the floor. Organizations have to be thoughtful and frame their message in a way that is relatable to everyone.

For example, consider a hospital that is getting shareholder pressure to reduce cost by 5 percent. The administration sends out an email telling everyone that their goal is to reduce cost by using fewer and cheaper materials. For a nurse on the floor, what does that mean? Is the nurse going to use one less swab to make the shareholders happy? Is the doctor going to push a drug because it's cheaper than the one she is currently administering? They won't, unless it meets their core value, which is patient care.

Furthermore, is reducing cost the real goal of the hospital? They may save 5 percent by taking a nurse off the floor or by using less material, but then workplace satisfaction would plummet along with the level of patient care. Saving 5 percent sometimes means losing far more.

After a year, the hospital realizes that while they reduced cost by 5 percent, they lost 6 percent in revenue. This year they decide they don't want to reduce cost and instead want to increase revenue by 5 percent. They inform the physicians that they will be seeing one more patient a day. Again, the level of care decreases and the optics are terrible—most hospitals avoid talking about profit.

If you are trying to align an organization's vision with the individual visions within the company, why even talk about 5 percent increase or reduction? It is not a goal that any of the staff is going to support without a ton of high-level information. Instead, leadership should frame their message to nest within the values of their team. How about, "Our goal is to improve patient satisfaction and care." If the hospital actually achieves that goal, their profits will increase. Furthermore, healthcare providers will be happy to provide even better care—it's why most of them went to medical school in the first place. To improve patient care is much more relatable to clients, as well. An organization has to create a vision that is exciting, that people can get behind, and that actually *relates* to the work being done.

Once an organization pins down its unified vision, strong leadership is mindful of how they choose to delegate. It can be tempting to cascade C-Suite goals down the organization and make someone else figure out how to implement the strategy. *I don't have time. They can sort it out for themselves.* It is tricky to delegate from a leadership perspective because there are two opposing ideas to contend with:

1. Someone on the floor should not be responsible for figuring out how to do cost-savings—that's what leadership is paid to do.

2. VP's rarely understand the ins and outs of their own organization. Someone on the floor might have a better understanding of what needs to happen than leadership does.

It can be tricky to marry those two ideas. RGI recommends leadership co-opt responsibility. Show your people that they are one of your core values by sitting down with project managers for a mere 15 minutes. Give them a list of five to ten ideas that the C-Suite thinks could work. Ask them to carefully look over them and choose one that makes the most sense. If none of them do, ask them what their solution would be. By offering someone a small amount of your time, you take a massive unknown off their table while getting relevant, practical feedback. And of course, the more buy-in the more acceptance; and the more collective genius, the more likely the vision is realized.

One of the best ways to motivate your people to buy-in to the organization's vision is to encourage positive action. The trick is, you have to encourage the *right* thing. Well thought-out motivation strategies can help bridge the gap between C-Suite goals and the rest of the team. They ensure that everyone is tracking toward the same goal.

Let's talk safety. Manufacturing companies emphasize safety for a good reason. They want every employee to go home safe to their family, friends, fishing boat (what have you). But, they often emphasize productivity, too—usually through a bonus structure. Leadership can shout, "Safety, safety, safety," while at the same time, rewarding potentially dangerous, fast-paced production. Not only have they undermined their own strategy, but they come across as disingenuous and hypocritical. As for the employee, should they go for the production bonus and take a risk with safety, or put safety first and give up the production bonus?

Instead, iX Leaders incentivize both. They create safety production bonuses, where team members receive a bonus barring any safety infractions. Or, they ensure that the safety gear is being used correctly and up to code. If it isn't, they buy new gear. Putting your money where your mouth is can be an incredibly influential form of non-verbal communication—no one will question where a company stands on safety when their gear is top notch and team members are sent to great training programs.

Furthermore, iX Leaders spend significant time on the floor. They personally assess what the riskiest job duties are and ask their team how they could make their job safer (and more productive! Safety and productivity aren't mutually exclusive). These leaders are mindful not to arbitrarily implement safety requirements that a.) don't make the work any safer, and b.), reinforce the notion that management is out-of-touch.

Remember, incentives are a form of communication that realign the vision of the organization with their people. Often, they are the most influential form. Whatever is incentivized becomes the number one priority for a team. That can become a real issue when leadership is saying one thing while promoting another. Strong leaders create cohesiveness by incentivizing the vision and values that they actually subscribe to.

WHAT'S FOR LUNCH?

Meg's Take:

A bunch of miners want a lunch shack, and no, this isn't the beginning of a really bad joke. Four times a year, mine technicians at a client company have the chance to talk to upper management with a singular, unified voice. They collectively bring up the most pressing issues on site in the hopes that leadership will address them. This time they didn't want much. They said, "We want a lunch shack."

"A lunch shack?"

Management looked at one another, a little amused. *We are trying to run a mining operation, and this is what they come up with? A lunch shack?*

The technicians clarified, saying "We want a warm place to eat a hot lunch."

"Um, we already have a cafeteria."

Embarrassed by management's reaction, they didn't push the idea further. Later, I asked a few technicians about the lunch shack, figuring it was about more than just a warm place to microwave a burrito.

"What's so important about the shack?"

152

"Every other field group has a place to eat a hot lunch." I realized this group was too far away to be trucking back to the main building to eat at the cafeteria. By not having a warm place to relax for a half hour on a 20 degree winter afternoon, they felt like they were not as valued as the rest of the team. From their perspective, management didn't care about them. That is a much bigger problem than cold coffee.

I realized these technicians weren't asking for anything fancy, so I did a little research. An insulated, portable shack with electricity and water would cost the company $12,000 to purchase and install. For an organization of their size, $12,000 was a small investment that would result in a high return: an entire group of workers being recognized as equal to the rest of the team. It would realign the technician's vision with the organization's by showing the technicians that they are being heard. When people feel like they are being heard, they are more likely to listen, and therefore, more likely to buy-in to your vision.

I don't recommend that leadership resolve every complaint. However, I do recommend investing in your team. When it's possible to make your employees' lives easier, don't give into the easy "no." If you put yourself out a bit for your people they'll respond with something you can't purchase: increased engagement and energy, better retention, improved optics, and ultimately, a strong iX. If our client had chosen to listen to their employees, they would have inspired loyalty.

TALKING VISION

"Don't ever let somebody tell you can't do something. Not even me. All right? You got a dream, you gotta protect it. People can't do something themselves, they wanna tell you can't do it. If you want something, go get it. Period."

Chris Gardner
The Pursuit of Happyness (2006)

153

It's extremely difficult to realize a vision when surrounded by people who don't share that vision. Imagine if the Wright brothers each thought the other one was crazy, both operating against one another. It can be surprising how people react to a new vision or aspiration. If you are thinking about telling someone about a new business plan, consider a few things about this person first:

- What is their Culture Type? Are they chaos-tolerant or order-tolerant?

 A Stabilizer isn't going to support you making a risky move that no one in your industry has yet to make—they care about your stability (financial well-being, stress levels, sanity, etc.) way too much for that. You might decide to tell this person once you have the ball rolling on the project and already have good news to report.

 An Organizer won't buy-in without the numbers. If your idea isn't well-researched or fully thought out, this person will likely pull it apart. Consider waiting to tell them until you can fully support your new venture with some data.

 A Fixer is going to start pointing out potential problem areas, making them great allies for new ideas—just be ready for some well-meaning critique.

 An Independent is generally a great Type to hash out wild ideas with. Settle in with a cup of coffee and a notebook, you might be there awhile.

- Where is this person in their career and how do they understand the industry?

- How is their personal life and mental state?

In order to become more than just an idea, your vision needs to be tended. From you, it needs excitement and energy, creative thinking, and hard work. From the people around you, it needs relevant criticism, enthusiasm, and honesty. A vision, in its infancy, is a delicate thing.

ACCOUNTABILITY

"Ninety-nine percent of all failures come from people who have a habit of making excuses."

George Washington Carver

Accountability is tricky because it's so easy to conceptualize, yet so difficult to implement. It can be problematic because it's a trait an individual chooses to demonstrate, and it isn't necessarily quantifiable. It can also be hard to accurately evaluate, since we rarely can know the true story. At one point or another, every leader puts their heads in their hands, unable to comprehend the destruction caused by a lack of accountability from a few individuals. That's what makes accountability so valuable to an organization and what makes it so challenging to inspire in others. That's why it's been a bestselling topic for the last half-century.

A strong iX built on the foundation of accountability means a culture that doesn't facilitate micromanaging. It means permission to ask when you need help without getting your head chopped off. It's the ability to proactively address issues before they result in disaster. It's the beginning of a truly team-based mindset.

IT'S ALL ABOUT "ME"-G

Meg's Take:

On the ranch, work doesn't start at nine and stop at five. You aren't afforded that luxury. Mother Nature has a way of making your schedule for you. When my dad asked me to help him take a cow to the vet the day before I left home for Creighton University, I wasn't surprised. I spent my last few hours of summer vacation transporting

156

that cow along dusty roads, watching the rows of corn disappear in the hot, South Dakota sun. I wondered if it would look the same in Nebraska.

Our veterinarian was a long-time friend of my dad's, Jason Mez. After the operation, Mez and I sat outside his office, passing the time talking about the heat and dry soil. Most South Dakotans consider crops and weather "small talk"—even if they live in the city.

Mez asked me what I planned on doing after high school, and I told him I was headed to college. He said, "Remember to take care of yourself." I rolled my eyes. It was the placating eye-roll of a "super confident" teenager who was scared as hell.

"Yeah, yeah...I'll be fine."

Jason Mez grew up without a father. He and his brothers worked through high school to help pay bills and buy meals. They attended the University of Nebraska and played football for the Huskers). After graduating, Mez quickly became a legend in the world of large animal medicine and had a knack for treating horses.

"No, I don't mean be careful. You know what my name and your name have in common? They both have the word 'me' in them. Meg and Mez. What I mean is this part of your journey is about *you*."

At the time, I thought it was a very weird thing to say. *Do I really need more self-confidence?* As a strong-willed and independent ranch kid, I seriously doubted it. I left for Creighton, and like most 18-year-olds, I immediately forgot all the advice I was given over the course of that summer. However, after I graduated and began to look at my life in reverse, I started thinking about Mez again. Finally, I could understand what he *actually* meant four years before: "You're responsible for your own success. Every day, it's up to you to make that happen.' Every day it *was* up to me. In college, every day I was responsible for the small things, like buying groceries and getting to class on time. In a grander sense, after leaving the ranch, I was responsible for my own fate. I was the only person who could define success for myself and the only person who could orchestrate it. I was finally at the point in my life where I could choose to make decisions or make excuses. I was learning how to stay accountable to myself.

Owning It

We all tend to be generous to ourselves and say, "I'm always accountable, other people are the problem." Then reality hits us, proving that we aren't, like ever. Becoming accountable is a hard transition to make, but imperative to adopting the iX Perspective and becoming a true iX Leader. The Personal Accountability Model, created by Mark Samuel, reveals there's a lot more to operating in the Accountability Loop or the Victim Loop than you might imagine.

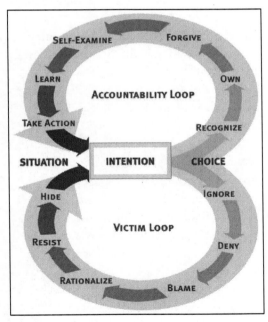

The Victim Loop is convenient, for a while. It allows us to pretend problems

158

don't exist. We ignore them, deny they are a problem, blame others, and rationalize issues under the rug. While it may feel like we're solving problems by stuffing them in a corner and promptly forgetting about their existence, we're making things worse. Those issues gain complexity and momentum while our backs are turned. When we are finally forced to face them, they are a much bigger issue than when they first occurred.

The better option is to live in the Accountability Loop and encourage your team to do the same. The Accountability Loop is about addressing problems head-on, as soon as they occur. It means owning problems, forgiving others, looking in the proverbial mirror and self-examining, learning from your mistakes, and taking action to solve the problem.

You'll notice from the Personal Accountability Model that everything begins with *choice*. When an issue occurs, we get to choose how we respond to it. We can own it, or we can deny it—the choice is ours. As we move through the cycle, we continue to make the choice to either continue on that path or leave it behind. Deciding that you have control over how you react in tough situations is one of the most critical steps leaders take in becoming an iX Leader.

It's important to note that you can move from loop to loop, even in one situation. Have you ever thought, "Man, I handled that really well," only to discover a couple weeks later that someone was still upset about the issue not being resolved? You may have recognized the issue, took ownership of it, but then slid down to rationalizing away some details or another person's ownership in the situation (holding others accountable is even harder than holding yourself accountable!).

Ok great, now that you read that section you'll be amazing at accountability! Buh-bye! Kidding. It takes lots of work to first convince yourself it's worth it, then break bad habits, and finally hold everyone else accountable. We've discovered a few tricks while implementing accountability in our own organization:

FOCUS ON THE WORK

It's easy to start blame-shifting and finger-pointing when the conversation is focused on "who" instead of "why." Keep the team's eye on how to improve in the future, as opposed to throwing colleges under the bus.

TALK IT OUT

Take the time to talk about what happened when goals aren't met. That doesn't mean dwell in the past, pass the blame torch around, or take turns explaining how each person goofed. It simply means to talk about what happened and make sure everyone feels good about moving forward. Encourage team members to think, blink, breathe, and move on.

FORGIVE

Forgiveness seems like a silly thing to think about. *Do I really need to forgive myself or others?* Yes. It doesn't matter how tough you are or how big your ego is—forgiving is the critical step we all miss when trying to move forward, and therefore, is the single biggest reason we don't move on from an issue. Sometimes it may even take saying the words out loud to yourself. *I forgive this person*, or *they're okay by me.* When you start to forgive people, you can grow in self-examination, education, and action.

CALL OUT EXCUSES

You may not be able to implement this one until the team is more comfortable with accountability and your leadership style, as it can seem like finger-pointing if everyone is not on board. Keep in mind, the delivery is also important. Calling out excuses is important because you want to make sure you aren't giving excuses a platform. If ignored, you and the team could easily be drug back down to the Victim Loop. You can say things like, "That sounds like an excuse, what is a solution?"

DOCUMENT RESULTS OF SUCCESS AND FAILURE

The human brain wants proof in order to continue following a protocol. That's why it's important to show that the Personal Accountability Model is working for the group. We're not proposing you hire a counselor to document each team member's feelings. Instead, have a chat with the group once in a while to say, "Boy, that went much more smoothly than before," or joke a little about almost falling into the Victim Loop. The more you talk about how things are working, the quicker the approach will be adopted by the group.

Meg's Take:
When people live in the Victim Loop, they tell themselves a lot of stories. Like most fiction, the story is realistic enough to for the audience to suspend their disbelief, or "to suspend one's critical faculties and believe something surreal." In other words, we are all capable of mastering the art of transforming reality into narrative. It only takes a little creativity to fashion a few white lies into a story that portrays you as the victim in your life.

I used to be the manager of Human Resources at a large company. I've heard a lot of fiction in my career. The stories began, "I wouldn't normally have called her an idiot, but I'm really stressed out because of the divorce," or "I never smoke in the cab, it was just cold out today, so I did this one time." Half reality (it was really cold), half fiction (this person smoked in the cab on hot days, too).

A few years ago, management tried implementing a new time clock system. It was simple: All employees had unique ID numbers to clock in and out. After an employee clocked in, they could also access to their current earnings and hours worked. Unfortunately, people kept forgetting their ID numbers, despite having them printed on a card that fit in a wallet. I heard all of the usual stories, like "I can't put my wallet in my coveralls because it might fall out." My personal favorite was a little more creative: "I keep my wallet with my phone, but it would be breaking company policy to have my phone in my pocket, so I just take them both out at the beginning of the day." Some of stories were rather elaborate.

Eventually, the foreman became so tired of having to look up everyone's numbers in the morning that he printed off a list of all employee names and numbers and placed it above the timeclock. His rationale went something like, "People need their numbers, and this way I don't have to look them up constantly." They had assumed no one would use someone else's number and misuse this information—why would they?

Soon after they taped the list to the wall I received a note informing me that Jeff clocked in under Jackie's number. Yep, you guessed it—Jeff had looked up her earnings and wage information. He walked over to Jackie and shouted, "You make more money than I do!" Then he went *back* to the time clock. Jeff continued to punch in other numbers, review their information, and share it with the rest of the team. You can imagine how unproductive the rest of the week was at that department.

When I called Jeff to my office for disciplinary action, I heard a very complex story that explained why it really wasn't his fault that he abused the system.

"Jeff, why would you look up your co-worker's information?"
"Well I didn't know."
"You didn't know what, exactly?"
"The foreman put the numbers out there."
"And that made it okay?"

162

"Well, um, probably not. But I don't care if anyone sees what I make."

"But does that make it okay?"

"This isn't a thing I would normally do, I never do this."

Jeff was suspended for a week without pay. Of course, not all of Jeff's story was complete fiction: The foremen made the first error by exposing people's personal information. They could have handled the situation in an infinite number of ways, but it was easier to say to themselves, "I'm the busiest person on site, I don't have time to babysit." That's just another story. A strong leader would recognize that Jeff wasn't the only one avoiding personal responsibility.

While holding ourselves and others accountable it's important to remember that the stories we tell ourselves are born in reality. The foremen are busy people, the compensation information was made available. The day she was late, it did actually snow. He is actually going through a divorce. Those issues deserve empathy because a person can't control the weather or traffic or other people. However, they can control how they view and interact with them. For example, it's okay to struggle to pay off debt. It's not okay to keep that from your partner. It's okay to drink soda and eat fried chicken wings. It's not okay to blame chickens and vegetable oil for a heart attack. You can't change reality, but you can change the way you and those around you perceive it.

LIVING IN CHOICE

"You are not born a winner,
You are not born a loser.
You are born a chooser."

Daymond John
American businessman, author, and motivational speaker

Rachel's Take:

In 2001, I need to lose some weight. When you're overweight you think to yourself, "I need to lose 20 pounds and eat better. I'm going to start exercising tomorrow." The next day you've got a gym membership and veggies in the fridge. You even start to see results. Then, for all kinds of valid reasons you don't totally commit, and inevitably fail.

Eventually, I experienced the catalyst I needed to do it—for real. I was in a Wal-Mart changing room trying on jeans. On the bench next to me were queen-sized panty hose I'd thrown in my cart moments earlier. I looked in the mirror as I squeezed my hips into a size 16. I hadn't picked out those jeans because I liked the style or the brand, I'd picked them out because they were the only thing on the shelf that I thought might fit. I wondered what it would be like to go into a store and have everything fit perfectly, but leave empty handed because, well, I just didn't like anything. I noticed my shoelace was untied and bent over. I gasped—out of breath, I sat down on the bench. Looking back at me in the mirror was a woman red-faced and winded from tying a shoelace. I decided she wasn't me—that was the first choice.

In choosing to not be her, I undertook one of the biggest projects of my life. In that dressing room, I made the choice to lose over 50 pounds and have been able to maintain that weight for 15 years. I've been able to stay true to my first choice by fashioning a system that would continuously inspire me to stay accountable to myself. For example, I started a Weight Watchers at Work program, where I was surrounded by people I knew. Suddenly, I wasn't anonymous. I had a group of people that were aware of what I wanted to achieve and could literally see whether or not I was succeeding. I stuck a sticky note outside my cubicle door every week after weigh-in, with the number of pounds I had lost. It was a badge of honor, a note of accomplishment. It was a metric of success (or failure) that I broadcasted to the 700-hundred-person office. I didn't have to do that; no one was forcing me to. However, making my intentions public continuously prompted me to stay accountable on days when I struggled.

Living in Choice means choosing to be accountable to yourself; to your goals, ambitions, health, and future. I'm not saying that anyone can just choose to be accountable and poof, like finding a genie in a bottle, all of their problems are gone. You can't wish away obesity or debt or a bad relationship. Not even close. Fifteen years ago, ten minutes in a dressing room was all the motivation I needed to know I was never going to be overweight again, but every hour of every day after I continued to make that choice.

If I don't work out today, it's because I choose to use my time in other ways, not because I'm "too busy." If I fail to achieve a goal, it's not because it was unrealistic, or I didn't work hard enough, or the clients didn't show up. It's because I didn't make it happen. If my life feels overwhelming, I can always go off to Jamaica and tend a beach-side bar while my kid plays in the surf. I choose to live the life I do. There is incredible freedom in making that choice.

Rewiring your brain to live in choice isn't a sprint. It's not a few weeks of intensive reflection and strict rules, it's a lifetime of it. Of course, I wouldn't advocate living in choice if it wasn't worth the effort. Living in choice, in business and in life, offers a richness and fullness that can only come to fruition through self-actualization and empowerment.

Meg's Take

When you're young, you think you're invincible, and that's true for a long time. Then you are put in a situation that you can't control. You are "reorganized," divorced, or bankrupt. You are forced into a change that you aren't prepared for. With time, you can look back at these moments with fresh eyes. Like watching an old movie, you can rewind and replay all the moments you put your heart into something or someone that didn't pan out, realizing it was doomed from the start. Your challenges and shortcomings are so painfully obvious in hindsight. The dramatic irony is that in every forgotten New Year's resolution, every failed investment, every disastrous relationship, there is one common denominator—*you*. Self-evaluation is disorienting and terrifying. Yet, it is incredibly empowering to know that you have real agency in your life. Ultimately, you are the problem and the solution. Now you can start to live in choice.

For me, Living in Choice sometimes looks like running. I genuinely love to run, but, like anything that's worth doing, it takes a lot effort. I have to continuously choose to train, so I stick to a regimen. At the start of this year, it was time for me to put together another program. While out for a run with my friend Dave, I mentioned that I wanted to get started. He asked,

"What's *your* race?"

"I'm gonna do a lot of races, what do you mean 'what's my race?'"

Dave looked at me. "You need to have *your* race, otherwise you won't do it." Dave was (annoyingly) right. Like sticking a Weight Watchers note on the outside of my door, I needed to prompt myself to live in choice. Without a goal in mind, I wouldn't meet my weekly miles. It would rain on Tuesday, I'd work late on Wednesday, my kids would catch a cold on Friday and all of the sudden the summer

166

would go by and I wouldn't be ready for any of the races I had imagined myself doing. Real and legitimate stories would eventually rob me of my fitness.

After talking to Dave, I signed up for the Missoula Marathon and paid a $90 entrance fee. Now when I'm tired and busy, I'll make time to train because my goal is real, achievable, in the immediate future, and I've made an investment toward it. In doing so, I've created a culture in which accountability is built into my system.

Unless we live in choice, we just stay spinning in the spot we are, terrified to get started because the first choice is so daunting. Instead, we continuously make the same excuses and do the same silly things over and over again. Albert Einstein is widely (and incorrectly) credited with the statement, "The definition of insanity is doing the same thing over and over again, but expecting different results." You won't see a change in your pattern until you make the choice to behave differently.

The magic of Living in Choice is in passion and energy, paired with someone or something to anchor you to it. The final ingredient is action. We call this mindset the G.S.D. (Get Shit Done) Triangle because it is the kind of mindset where a person decides on a goal, vision, or New Normal and achieves it—period.

If you are going to change, you have to remind yourself why you're passionate about that change. If Rachel wasn't completely ready to lose weight, she wouldn't have. If I wasn't passionate about running, I wouldn't train. Passion for something gives you the energy you need to achieve it. Passion keeps you driven and motivated. If you have passion and energy, then all you need is someone or something to help you stay accountable to it, or anchor you to it. For Rachel it's her health—for me it's my girls.

An anchor has to be something that's powerful enough to keep you accountable when things get tough. It has to help you visualize your New Normal and push you into the Let Go. An anchor allows you to say "no" to one more cigarette or "yes" to one more lap around

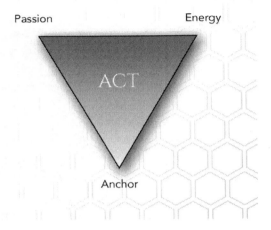

Passion   Energy

ACT

Anchor

the track when all you want to do is give up. When I don't want to train I remind myself of my anchor: My girls are watching. They can either watch their mother demonstrate a healthy lifestyle and meet goals and complete marathons, or they can watch their mother give up and take they easy way out. Of course, passion, energy, and an anchor are nothing without action. Nothing convinces me to take action and throw on my running shoes like remembering that I am accountable to my daughters.

THE MIRROR

Staying accountable is a little like ordering a kale salad while meeting your girlfriend's parents for the first time. Before leaving the house, you throw on a sharp blazer and brush your teeth. You brainstorm topics on the drive to the restaurant to avoid any awkward silences. Once there, you have a drink to calm your nerves. The server comes back and you order a kale salad, remembering her parents are vegetarian. Nice. Another drink. The next hour flies by and you head to the restroom before leaving. You grin as you walk. While washing your hands and congratulating yourself on being so likable, you look up at the mirror and…damn. You have something green ever-so-determinedly caught between your teeth—face smashed against the mirror and fingers jammed in your mouth, all you do is manage to wedge it on in there even further. On the drive home, your girlfriend rolls her eyes at the at-least-three times you called her dad, Roger, Robert, and reminds you that her mom is an ophthalmologist, not an optician (you'll be Googling the difference later).

That night you lay awake in bed, replaying the dinner over and over in your head. *I was more nervous than I thought.* You try to write a version of the story where you aren't making a fool out of yourself. There isn't one.

Defeated, the next morning you pull together the courage to call up her parents and apologize. It's a little painful, like putting lotion on a sun burn. At least the apology is better than obstinately laying out in the sun, rotating back and forth on a towel like a cut of meat on a barbecue. You and Roger end up having a good laugh about the whole thing, and before hanging up the phone you manage to make plans to get together next week. You'll make sure it goes better this time.

It takes grit to recognize when you've missed the mark, it takes courage to own up to it. A true leader forgoes cheap rationalization and justification—they know when they are wrong. Taking time to look in the proverbial mirror and see yourself reflecting humility is the ability to "lead by example." Show your team that you can stay accountable both to yourself and to them, and they will return it tenfold. It takes an incredible amount of integrity, and often times an incredible sacrifice, to give and receive respect through accountability.

From a leadership perspective, inspiring accountable teams means enabling leadership and staff with the courage to face minor setbacks head on before they become full-on disasters. The Unspoken Conversations that result destroy iX. Minor misalignments, disagreements, and misunderstandings are often ignored until they become big ugly issues that come with hurt feelings, bruised egos, and barely suppressed anger. The actions that result, of course, are a withdrawal from the team, dismissive or argumentative relationships, and spiteful backstabbing (which boils down to a lack of respect for each other).

Part of the reason Unspoken Conversations never come to light is that conflict is something that most people avoid at all costs. How many times have you decided to turn a blind eye, thinking "I'll just let that go, maybe it will sort itself out."?

Lots of times, we know.

How often does it sort itself out?

Probably never. And thus, an Unspoken Conversation is born.

Entire philosophies have grown up around conflict resolution, conflict management, and conflict avoidance. Any concept that excuses leaders from having hard conversations misses the boat entirely. Conflict only *feels* awkward and uncomfortable when parties involved fail to address issues immediately. However, we aren't encouraging leaders to babysit their teams, meaning teams and individuals have just as much of a responsibility to address internal conflict as leadership.

It's well worth the effort to deal with Unspoken Conversations—they are a killer of iX. The good news is they are surprisingly easy to avoid. We like to think of them like a marathon runner getting ready for a race. Marathon runners (like Meg) know that they have to run consistently. They can't just put in one solid month of running and then plop down on their couch the next month—they are training for the long game. That's why most people can't just line up in the chilly predawn on a Saturday morning and gut out 26.2 miles (while the rest of us mortals are enjoying our warm beds). However, a lot of mere mortals could line up for a 5K (3.1 miles) and at least finish the thing (although they might not look like a million bucks afterward). The point is that the bigger the run, the more energy and time it takes to prepare for and deal with it successfully.

iX Leaders apply the same principles to Unspoken Conversations. If you deal with issues immediately, it doesn't take much energy to solve them. You chat for a few minutes, sort out a solution, or resolve the miscommunication, and everyone goes on with their lives. Assuming you aren't a masochist, you'd rather run the 5K than the marathon, right? The longer an Unspoken Conversation goes ignored the more energy and time it takes to resolve it.

Our solution? Fix it right damn now.

And this goes for other performance, productivity, or gut-feel weirdness issues.

If a leader addresses problems immediately with an even hand and reasonable approach, then that empowers others in the team to do the same. Remember, Stabilizers, the largest Culture Type, want to see leaders emulating what they themselves are expected to do. That old "Do what I say, not what I do" parenting technique (which we both use, particularly when it comes to "adult language") does not work in the office.

It takes courage to address issues head-on. Of course, when you do, hairy issues and challenges become manageable. Maybe production numbers are low or a schedule has fallen behind or Suzie is upset because she didn't get the raise she was hoping for. Address those issues immediately and inspire your team to do the same.

The longer you or your team let things go, the longer you operate in fear. In fact, if you operate in fear too long, then crappy attitudes and a miserable iX can become the New Normal. Issues become critical when they go on so long that they introduce increasing risk into the project, be it risk to goals, productivity, the bottom line, or iX. Catastrophic issues occur when those challenges become devastating to the business at large. Businesses can fail and have failed because they haven't addressed issues in the early stages.

If a leader has a great team, then they can often allow their internal team to handle manageable issues. The last thing we want to encourage is micromanagement (ugh!). But, leaders do have to set an example and keep an eye out for Unspoken Conversations that reach a boiling point (you know the ones).

However uncomfortable it feels to have those Unspoken Conversations, that exchange between leader and team is necessary to create an accountable culture where everyone has the confidence to be transparent.

REAL-TIME ACCOUNTABILITY

Rachel's Take:

The Landsat satellite imaging program is an epic, 40-plus year mission that's made a significant contribution to the scientific understanding of Earth. In 1972, Landsat 1 (originally called Earth Resource Technology Satellite, or ERTS-1) was the first civilian spacecraft ever launched with the goal of imaging the earth's surface for scientific study. Humankind could now look at Earth in a new way, with regularity, and in portions of the electromagnetic spectrum that changed our understanding of the planet. Landsat satellites 2, 3, 4, and 5 were launched in fairly regular intervals through 1984, when Landsat 5 achieved orbit with an expected lifespan of around three years. Landsat 6 is resting at the bottom of the Pacific Ocean, covered with 25 years of marine snow. She landed there in 1993, after the rocket designed to push her through Earth's gravitational pull malfunctioned.

A satellite mission, once launched and nominally operating, requires an impressive and comprehensive team that is broken down into distinct areas of responsibility. The team at the ground station uplinks command loads to the birds, downlinks data from their onboard recorders, and conducts live acquisitions with the big receiving dishes. The ground station also archives and processes the data, ensures health and safety, disseminates data, and monitors sensor acquisition. The flight ops team develops the actual commands that are uploaded to the spacecraft and determines which images to acquire. There are also teams of engineers and scientists who are distributed throughout academic and Federal institutions that have some level of interest, commitment, or dependence upon the mission. The scope of the operation is remarkable.

I know so much about Landsat because in 2007 I was hired as the new Data Acquisition Manager for Landsats 5 and 7. It was apparent from day one that Landsat would not only be one of the largest teams I've worked with, but also the highest performing. We all had to be accountable to each other—if one team came up short, the entire mission would suffer.

One of those teams was Calibration and Validation. It was their responsibility to constantly check the images to ensure the satellites were behaving in a way that was expected. When there was an inconsistency or issue with the images, they were the first people to know. In fact, they had to have eyes on an image within 24 hours.

At one of the first meetings I attended it was clear that Calibration and Validation was taking too long to assess data after downlinking. The project manager, we'll call her Susan, sat us all down around the table. She looked at Zach, the project manager of Calibration and Validation.

"Why is this image assessment not being completed on time?" she asked.

Zach looked flustered. "We've slowed down our process because we are supporting the test phase of the new release of the processing system."

Susan was concerned, but she also understood that Zach was trying to manage many competing priorities. Together, they would have to sort out how to accomplish both objectives: Support testing while providing image review. The image review took priority because it was one the ways to diagnose sensor or spacecraft malfunction. Landsat 7 had a significant malfunction in 2003, and it was a near-mission-ending problem.

Susan could have gotten upset or taken Zach into an adjacent room and had a "closed door" conversation. Instead, she chose to be transparent by addressing all parties affected. This was a genius move on her part—everyone heard the rationale and follow-on discussion of what needed to be changed. It gave Zach a chance to make sure that Susan fully understood the complexities of the requirements. No one talked about it later in the break room. No one questioned who was and wasn't on the right track. When issues are addressed as soon as they appear you avoid escalating conflict and misunderstanding, echoed in the Marathoner's Curve above. Everyone left the meeting knowing exactly where they fit in the Landsat mission and why their work was so valuable.

Transparency

"In a communication vacuum, people will just make shit up."
Dr. Rachel MK Headley

Transparency is a mechanism by which entire companies stay accountable to themselves, their work force, and their clients/consumers. If a company makes its goals and values public, as well as the way in which is meets those goals, then people can see a system of accountability built into an organization—one they can trust. Transparency is a company's way of saying, "We believe in our business and our product, and we trust the public to hold us accountable to our own standards."

Transparency battles misinformation. It takes the "he said, she said," out of a discussion and replaces it with fact. The human population generates at least 2.5 quintillion bytes of data a day. If your organization is big enough to be on the radar, that means that some of that data will be about you. If an anonymous blogger is going to write about your company anyway, why not have the facts readily available? Furthermore, the idea of transparent business practices emerging from a culture amidst an onslaught of fake news is rather refreshing. Transparency won't keep people from lying, but it will ensure that the truth is always available for those who seek it.

Transparency creates room for communication, and therefore speeds up all facets of an organization. When individuals, or even entire divisions, in are siloed from each other, things happen more slowly. That's in part because when a mistake is made, no one feels confident in speaking up. If a company instead chooses to be transparent, it builds a work culture where team members feel comfortable to share their ideas and critique each other. That's where innovation starts.

Transparency inspires loyalty from your team by making your organization inclusive. When a company shares information with its team, it makes them a part of the vision, as opposed to a workhorse in the nine to five grind. In being transparent, an organization gives every individual the tools to solve their own problems, the opportunity to think about the company critically, and the agency to create something to be proud of. Transparency allows employees to take figurative ownership in the company, and ownership not only inspires integrity and quality of work, but a culture where leaders trust that employees will put forth their best effort. Employees who work in a transparent environment are more engaged, more productive, interact with consumers in a more positive way, and are more willing to stay even if a new opportunity or different job offer arises.

Organizations are expected by the public and their team to have a greater level of transparency than ever before— a major paradigm shift over the last decade. Information used to be disseminated on a "need to know," "top down" basis. Today, according to Forbes Magazine, 25 percent of privately held companies share financial information with all of their employees. That's up from just 7 percent only four years ago.

Transparency is linked to employee satisfaction, which just so happens to be one way in which RGI diagnoses an organization's iX. Research suggests that transparent organizations are satisfied ones. TINYpulse, a software company whose mission is to increase employee happiness, notes that "management transparency is the top factor when determining employee happiness...with an extremely high correlation coefficient of .93 with employee happiness."

Other numbers support this claim. Buffer, a social media management company, received 1,623 more applications for job openings after only a month of making every salary completely transparent. In an interview with Quartz (Atlantic Media's digital news outlet), co-founder Joel Gascoigne stated, "We've never been able to find great people this quickly in the past."

Buffer not only publicizes salaries, but also publicizes their formula for determining wages. According to Buffer, their radical level of transparency alleviates employee anxiety around income. When a future team member sits down for an interview, they know exactly how much they will earn. Even better, they know *why* they will earn that amount. Having a public formula that assigns wages based on a transparent system that, by design, cannot discriminate or hold prejudice is a smart and honest way to do business.

SumAll has been disclosing employee wages since its first day of business in the form of Google Docs. Apptopia has a bank of monitors that line the walls of the lobby, displaying monthly revenues and customer churn. Zappos' core value is to "Build Open and Honest Relationships with Communication." They achieve this in part by allowing Q&A with customer service, user experience, and marketing, as well as offering tours of the facility.

Patagonia has created their entire brand around global responsibility and transparency. Their website displays every factory, textile mill, and farm marked on an interactive map. Click on a mill and you'll know how many workers are currently employed, what's being produced, and what measures they are taking to reduce their environmental impact.

To reap benefits from increased transparency, you don't have to be as radical as Buffer or Patagonia. You can improve productivity and employee morale just by making goals and expectations clear. TINYpulse analyzed 40,000 responses from over 300 companies around the world. According to their survey, only 42 percent of employees know their organization's vision, mission, and values. The results, while surprising to some, reinforce what we have seen over and over in our client businesses.

Greater transparency means a happy, productive workforce. This is true in part because transparency builds trust, and people want to engage with a company they can trust. Today the workforce and consumers alike can choose more than just a paycheck or a product; they can choose to support a company whose ethical standards match their own.

Consumer and employee demand for transparency in the workplace aren't going away. If anything, they are growing louder and stronger. It's up to businesses to modernize and adapt to consumer needs. Before shrugging off the value of transparency, consider the heat Facebook is currently taking from not being transparent about data mining (again). Consider the scrutiny that promotional tags like "local," "GMO free," and "fair trade" now receive after a history of implying one thing, and then doing another. Better yet, consider the optics of what 24/7 Wall Street news outlet calls "America's Most Hated Companies":

- Monsanto is currently in class-action lawsuit alleging that exposure to the company's popular weed killer, Roundup, causes cancer.

- Comcast charged customers for unauthorized services and equipment.

- Wells Fargo employees created millions of fake accounts without customers' knowledge.

- Equifax waited a month and a half to publicly state they had suffered one of the largest data breaches of all time.

- Cigna inflated medical costs, causing some customers to pay as much as 10 times the true cost of their medical services.

There are many explanations as to why these companies have poor optics, but an unmistakable common thread is lack of transparency.

Now that consumers are more educated on the products they buy and can choose where they spend their dollar, they have more power than ever before. They want to support companies they can trust, and therefore companies have to revolutionize the way they have been disseminating information. Writer and journalist Rebecca Solnit argues that in a revolution, once something is created it can't be un-created, or once Pandora's box is opened, the contents can't go back in the box. She writes, "What doesn't go back in [Pandora's] jar or the box are ideas. And revolutions are, most of all, made up of ideas." Business transparency is a box that has been opened, and one that that isn't going to close.

EMPATHY

"At its very heart, a business is the beauty of bringing together people and things to make the community better off—these are the businesses we admire. Empathy is the one tool that makes it all happen."

Angel Cabrera
President of George Mason University

Empathy is often misunderstood as a "soft" trait. In reality, empathy is essential to powerful leadership. That's because empathy paired with accountability creates teamwork. We don't mean *team* as in a group of people brought together to work on a project—instead we mean the kind of high-functioning, ultra-productive team that can create something truly amazing, like the folks at Google or the team responsible for GE's new clean technology. It's time to forget preconceived notions that empathetic people are soft-hearted "do-gooders" or incapable of being powerful leaders.

Of course, a leader can't lead with empathy alone—it also takes accountability to lead a team. An organization based solely on empathy results in weak-willed leadership, with the end result being entirely unimpressive. When a leader is a push-over, not only will nothing get done, but the hardest workers and biggest achievers will no longer be motivated. Nothing zaps motivation faster than a leader who believes "good enough" is acceptable and "you did your best" means success. This approach to leadership will always end up tossed on the trash heap of failed good intentions.

We demand excellence through accountability. However, accountability without empathy is totalitarianism. If you only lead with accountability, in the simplest of terms your staff won't like you. Whether or not you care is irrelevant—what does matter is their performance. Think about someone you dislike, compared to someone you admire. Which of the two people are you going to go the extra mile for? Who do you respect, and who do you want to be respected by? If a leader only leads through accountability, the bottom line will be poor in quality and quantity. Don't bet on that team sticking around when a better opportunity arises, either.

Ideally, an organization operates in the nexus of accountability and empathy. That's because we've realized that empathy is an incredibly effective tool to make just about everything and anything run smoothly. From finding out why an initiative didn't stick to holding meetings in the board room; to evaluating perspectives and tough negotiations with clients and partners, empathy paired with accountability is the grease in the gears of a winning organization. In the sweet spot between accountability and empathy, iX Leadership fosters a sense of comradery and pride that can't be bought or coerced. Staff becomes team, workers become people, and bosses become leaders.

Empathy + Accountability

"Leadership is providing mechanisms and safe platforms by which your people can be brave enough to be accountable."

Meg Manke

Leading means balancing empathy and accountability. If a leader is too empathetic, they run the risk of missing the bottom line. If a leader employs micromanagement in an effort to maintain control over every last detail or has a take-no-prisoners attitude toward mistakes, that leader will fail their people miserably. It's a tricky recipe to follow, but if used in the right proportions, empathy and accountability can motivate a team to accomplish incredible things.

Our advice is to set high expectations, then ensure your team has everything they need to meet them. Johann Wolfgang von Goethe famously said, "If I accept you as you are, I will make you worse;
180

however, if I treat you as though you are what you are capable of becoming, I help you become that." A high expectation, in of itself, inspires accountability. Humans have a fundamental drive to succeed. We love being good at things—especially at our work. The empathy half of this equation is making sure your team has everything they need to meet those expectations. If you set your team up to fail, they will. As a leader, you have to ensure their needs are met.

An iX Leader is empathetic to the traits of each Culture Type we outlined in Part I. As demonstrated in the story above, perceptive leaders manage employees with equal respect and a tailored approach. For example, an Independent might feel micromanaged and suffocated by a manager that a Stabilizer absolutely loves. An Organizer might feel annoyed or even overwhelmed by a dynamic, *chaos-tolerant* approach that a Fixer will thrive in. It's leadership's job to understand their team by familiarizing themselves with the different needs and strengths of each Culture Type.

While each Culture Type is supported by different messages, an important aspect of balancing accountability with empathy is remembering that everyone needs to feel valued. Offering the right amount of control, respect, and support says, "I care about you, and I care about the business. How can we make both work together?" That is the secret sauce for creating the kind of behavior that allows for employee happiness, creativity, and innovation.

Michael didn't have a college degree or formal education and supported his family with his hourly position as a welder at a machine shop. Yet, in just five years he had worked his way into a high level, salaried position. It more than doubled his income for his family and drastically changed their life. The company was excited to promote him—he was well liked by everyone and leadership thought he would do well with more responsibility.

He had been working as the new shop foreman for five months when he came into Human Resource's office to talk.

"I'm not cut out for this," he said.

Jim, head of HR, and Michael's supervisor, Mary, were baffled. He was so qualified. Jim asked, "What aren't you comfortable with?"

"I'm stressed out."

"What's stressing you out?"

"I'm not really sure what the expectations are."

After that conversation, Michael and Mary met every day to review the job duties and requirements. Mary sat down and spelled it all out for him. Deadlines were set, expectations were clear, examples were given. Eventually they backed off to weekly meetings, but Mary continued to coach Michael regularly.

In six months, Michael was back in Jim's office. Jim could tell Michael was nervous; he shuffled his feet and looked at his desk while he spoke.

"I really appreciate all that you and the company have done for me. But, if there is an hourly position that comes back up, I would love the opportunity to have it."

Jim looked at him for a while, unsure of what to say. Mary was livid. Over the last nine months the company had offered to pay for him to get a degree in engineering or business. They were willing to accommodate his class schedule so he could have an income while in school. They were happy to send him to leadership training. The company was so invested in his success they'd have given him just about anything he asked for.

It was hard enough for Michael to realize the position was the wrong fit for him. Mary unintentionally made it harder. Let me explain. For Mary, success meant a higher salary and a higher position on the org chart. She couldn't understand why Michael would choose stability and certainty over that. He failed to employ the Mad Hatter Principle (see page 184) and felt angry at Michael for not taking advantage of this opportunity.

In the end, as a Stabilizer Michael was a Culture Type mismatch to the role. We can all work outside of our "home" Culture Type for a while, but over time a mismatch can cause anxiety and stress. If left unchecked, that stress will make someone seek another position, as was the case for Michael. Perhaps if Jim understood Culture Types he would have been able to empathize with Michael better, and even tailor the role to suit his Type.

However, I want to make it clear that there are plenty of Stabilizer leadership roles. The issue in Michael's case was that Mary was treating Michael like a *chaos-tolerant* teammate (like himself). Jim had no idea how to accommodate the south half of our graph. Mary (a Fixer) needed five minutes, two rubber bands and a lighter to MacGyver a new plan. Mary failed to offer Michael the time he needed to process the transition. Furthermore, Mary failed to make a full list of resources available to Michael.

The question is, could Michael have stayed in his position if leadership had a strong iX, meaning they understood how to use accountability, empathy, and Culture Types effectively? Or, was it that Michael should have known he wasn't suited to the role and not accepted the position in the first place? There are some illuminative lessons in Michael's story that answer those questions.

First, as an applicant considering a position, know what that role entails. Is it a team-based role? Will you be working alone? Will you have to critique or be at odds with your co-workers? Does the role have a lot of variation? How do you feel about that variation—is it chaos, or freedom? If the role isn't perfect, what is the duration? Taking the time to answer those questions is some of the best advice we have for evaluating a role before you sign on for it.

Second, if the person didn't ask themselves the questions above, or they decided that the positives outweighed the negatives and accepted a mismatched role, it doesn't necessarily mean it won't work in the long run. However, it **does require a different approach.** For Mary, this means altering the role to better suit Michael's Type. Mary could have proactively assessed the job requirements that a Stabilizer would struggle with and modified them ahead of time. For example,

Mary could have rolled out the transition more slowly, giving Michael more time to adapt to his new role. Mary also could have provided alternative feedback, emphasizing the team benefits and stability that Michael's promotion had created. When it comes to adapting roles based on Type, a little empathy can go a long way toward making a team member feel more comfortable, and ultimately more successful.

While this highlights an order-tolerant person moving into a *chaos-tolerant* role and struggling to adapt, the inverse is also true. We hear of this Culture Type mismatch in Sales leadership quite often. The very best salesperson gets promoted into a VP of Sales position. Guess what? The Independent salesperson struggles, and may even whither, under the repetitive and detail-oriented nature of the VP role. They don't like it, are likely less skilled at it than others, and may end up leaving the organization.

MAD HATTER PRINCIPLE

"Why is a raven like a writing desk?"
"Have you guessed the riddle yet?" the Hatter said, turning to Alice again.
"No, I give it up," Alice replied. "What's the answer?"
"I haven't the slightest idea."

Alice in Wonderland
Lewis Carroll
Tim Burton, 2010 version

The origin of the term "mad as a hatter" can be traced back to 1829, when hatters used a solution containing mercuric nitrate to smooth animal furs for felting. Eventually these furs became felts by repeatedly boiling them in water and drying. During the felting process, the volatile free mercury assaulted hatter's lungs and bare skin, and over time they contracted erethism, or mercury poisoning. Symptoms of erethism include tremors, wild mood swings, an unpredictably short temper, and what was described at the time as "bashfulness." Over time, these bizarre symptoms became synonymous with the hat industry and the term "Mad Hatter" was coined.

Like the real hatters of London, Carroll's Hatter behaves strangely. Those who are familiar with the work (or at least the movie), are aware that the Hatter's antics aren't nearly as strange as how the rest of the Tea Party reacts to them. No one, apart from Alice, is offended or even surprised when he prattles off riddles and jumps around the table. Why? Because the Tea Party knows better than to take his behavior at face value, they allow him some grace, because he might not make sense at first blush. We use this analogy to encourage the same behavior in our leaders—to develop a skill to see beyond surface-level behavior to seek the root cause of issues, concerns, and challenges.

The Mad Hatter Principle states that leaders should extend the same grace the Tea Party gives the Hatter by assuming your team is always well intentioned, even if you might suspect nefarious intent. This principle recommends you consider all other possibilities for questionable behavior before making dangerous assumptions. For example, chronic tardiness can seem irresponsible on the surface. However, this person could lack reliable transportation or be taking care of a sick child. You don't know until you ask.

Rachel's Take:

We all tend to see the world from our own point of view, especially when we're young. When I was growing up none of us could see beyond who had the right outfit, who had the best car, and who got to stay out the latest. Ugh. That kind of self-absorbed, naive, and narrow perception left all of us confused and alienated. From my equally limited vantage, it felt like people were out to get me—or worse, ignore me completely.

I did have one weapon against teenager-dom that helped me make it through that oh-so-judgmental and highly-intense time. I had the Mad Hatter Principle (although it would be over two decades before Meg and I put a name to it). Because I had moved around a lot between 4th and 8th grades, I had learned that most people are so wrapped up in their own story, fears, and insecurities that pre-teens and teens scarcely noticed those around them. I began to realize that it wasn't that I was a leper, it was more that everyone else was so worried about their own gig that I went unnoticed.

When you are stressed or busy and someone does something that inconveniences or offends you, it is easy to attack their character. When your barista takes ten minutes to make you a latte instead of the breve you asked for, he is careless and intentionally making you late for a meeting. When your co-worker is late for the third time this week, she is inconsiderate (maybe) and shirking her responsibilities (possibly). And that neighbor with the dog that barks every night at 2 a.m.? He is unequivocally the worst human in the world with zero chance for redemption (this might, in fact, be true).

The problem with assuming nefarious intent or poor character is that negative reactions don't help either party achieve anything. Your barista isn't going to re-make your drink any faster because you were rude to him. Instead, you turned out to be the jerk as you loudly demanded half and half instead of milk or refused to tip. Your co-worker is probably not going to be more prompt when you roll your eyes behind her back or complain about her at lunch. That passive aggressive note you left on your neighbor's door? Eh, we'll leave the dog out of this. One thing is certain: all you've managed to do is create an environment in which both parties are upset, and the situation never improves.

The Mad Hatter Principle is much more powerful than just a way to get along with others. It's really a gift you give yourself in that it replaces your anger and frustration with empathy. When you allow yourself to presume that the person sitting across from you is a good person that is trying to do the right thing, suddenly all of your built-up irritation or resentment disappears and is replaced with curiosity. You relax and ask yourself, "what is the real reason they are acting this way?" Suddenly you are in a position to help fix a problem because you gained a greater awareness of what is actually wrong. Fixers and Independents are naturally inclined to this challenge. Organizers and Stabilizers can learn to love it, especially if they employ the Experience Cube (see page 194) alongside the Mad Hatter Principle. Using these two methods in tandem gives Stabilizer-Organizers a method to help further analyze a situation.

Meg's Take:

Our dachshund, Ginger, was born in Missouri. I live in Spearfish, South Dakota. Logically, the breeder and I decided we would meet somewhere in the middle to swap a check for a puppy.

"Sioux Falls at ten?"

"Sioux Falls at ten!" I responded.

Rachel and I hopped in the car, totally puppy-prepared: blanket, kennel, puppy snacks, excited kids, the whole thing. I couldn't wait to see the look on my girls' faces when Ginger got in the car. Five and a half hours later, at 9:45, we were in Sioux Falls, South Dakota. When 10:15 came around, I got a text from the breeder.

"Where are you? I'm at Exit 145."

Rachel and I looked at each other.

"There isn't an exit 145 in Sioux Falls," I said.

At the same time, all three of us realized that she was an hour and a half south, in Sioux City, which sits on the Iowa/South Dakota border.

Regardless of who was supposed to be where, I knew arguing about it wasn't going to magically transport one of us to the other's location, so instead I said,

"Vermillion is halfway between Sioux City and Sioux Falls. Let's meet there!"

Although the breeder was clearly frustrated, she finally agreed, and I gave her some basic directions and off we went.

By the time we met up in Vermillion, her attitude had totally changed. She was warm and friendly, and even said that it only ended up adding an extra twenty minutes to her drive. I could have mirrored her earlier frustration and bickered about where we were supposed to meet up, but that obviously wouldn't have gotten us anywhere. Furthermore, when someone is stressed and anxious, mirroring their stress and anxiety only magnifies it. The beauty of employing the Mad Hatter Principle is that all of us left happy.

There is a scientific reason as to why the Mad Hatter Principle doesn't come naturally to all of us. According to Chris Hopwood, associate professor of Psychology at Michigan State University and Director of the Michigan State University Psychological Clinic, the issue lies in what is called "complementarity." Complementarity suggests that we tend to respond in a way that complements another person's actions.

According to Hopwood, there are two main veins of complementarity. The first is a sort of mirroring, where "warmth begets warmth and coldness begets coldness." For example, if someone is rude to you at the grocery store, you are most likely going to be rude back, and vice versa. The second avenue is a leader-follower dynamic. Or, as Hopwood phrases it, "Dominance begets submission whereas submission begets dominance." When someone takes charge and assumes a powerful leadership role, it is natural to follow. For example, when you're on a hike with a friend and take a wrong turn, a dominant response would be to look at the map and say, "I know where we are, let's go this way." When your friend nods their head in agreement, they are acting submissively toward dominance. The inverse is true as well. If you had instead said, "Would you please look at the map, I don't know where we are," and your friend responded, "Sure, I can get us back on track," you acted submissively and your friend responded dominantly.

Complementarity takes the path of least resistance. As Hopwood explains, "If someone is nice to you, you tend to be nice back. If they're not nice, then why should you be? If someone seems to know what they are doing, it is natural to follow. And when you are in charge, it is easiest if others do what you say." Complementarity is what usually feels like the most natural response to someone's behavior.

Non-complementary behavior is exactly what you'd expect: It occurs when someone breaks the pattern of complementarity by responding in an unexpected way, with generally negative results. When two people both act submissively, they aren't very effective. When two people are both dominant, they tend to argue more than is necessary. When someone is kind and another person rude, it is obviously…off-putting. However, when a person is initially impolite and someone responds with kindness, the entire dynamic of the relationship can shift. That is when non-complementary behavior can benefit you and is the very essence of the Mad Hatter Principle.

Rachel's Take:

We realize that in theory, the Mad Hatter Principle sounds great. We know that in reality, there are bad actors. We debate this between ourselves a lot. I always say, "There are no jerks!" to which Meg always responds, "Sure, but what about when they act like jerks?" It's important to remember that the Mad Hatter Principle only works up to a point. When there really is a bad actor on your team, there are two potential outcomes: leadership will remove them or they'll remove themselves. That individual has to decide if they are up or out. The employee has two choices: Step up and become accountable, or be taken out of the organization. As a leader, it's your responsibility to help guide that transition, and be receptive if they choose to step up.

BUSINESS IS PERSONAL

"Business is always personal. It's the most personal thing in the world."
Michael Scott
The Office

Rachel's Take

Last year, I found myself working with a great team that was struggling to implement a new change. The project manager, Wes, acted strangely during our first videoconference. He was cagey and closed off. Later, when I met him face to face, he had a hard time meeting my eyes, and when he spoke, it was short and to the point. Initially, I wrote it off as a personality quirk.

The next day, Wes was scheduled to introduce me at an all-hands meeting. I braced myself for what I assumed would be a lukewarm and rather awkward introduction. On the contrary, Wes was a great speaker in front of his team. He was engaging and vibrant, well-spoken and inspiring. After his speech, he looked over at me to welcome me onstage. I tried (and likely failed) to hide my surprise.

After some work with his team, we met to go over the report I had created for him. It started out like other meetings I had with Wes—back to being weirdly closed off. So, I started my message by saying that I thought his people were great, and that he was doing a great job developing his teams (which was true). His body language immediately opened up, and he was much more engaged throughout the entire conversation.

Wes oversaw a great team because as a Stabilizer leader, he was incredibly engaged with and proud of his team. I suspect he was worried that I would directly critique his *personal* leadership style, and by extension, his team. Eventually, I realized that Wes didn't have a problem with me, but instead was taking my critique personally.

That's why when I complimented his team, he immediately engaged with me. Remember, business is always personal.

EMPATHY AS STRATEGY

"You're going to find out one day, it's harder to be kind than clever."
Grandfather of Jeff Bezos,
CEO of Amazon

Rachel's Take:

When I asked Meg Manke to jump into business with me, I knew I was setting myself up to wait. Though she had always dreamed of working for herself and she was almost in a position to make the leap, I knew the transition wasn't going to be instantaneous. She currently had a big-time, full-time job with a title, benefits, and the security and prestige that go with it. When considering the KCTM, I knew that even though she wanted to join me, a change of this magnitude would likely take years to normalize.

We worked on our IP for a long time before I asked her to partner with me and busied ourselves by conducting research and evaluating options. At this time, I was working on my own (keeping my head above water and hoping she'd take some work off of my plate soon) while she continued working at her corporate job. It was a situation rife with the possibility of misunderstanding and frustration.

About eight months after asking her to partner, I requested (*ahem!* *demanded*) she set a date for her last day at her J-O-B. She finally picked a deadline of November 20th. I needed that deadline as much, or more, than she did. However, I noticed that the closer we came to November 20th, the less and less she spoke of her upcoming departure. I had a hunch she was going to blow past it. What was a mystery to me at that time was whether or not she would ever leave,

191

and, if she would, when? During this transitional period I had a lot of doubts.

Why won't she fully commit?
Why am I carrying the burden?
Is she ever going to leave?
Am I wasting my time?
Will this ever work?!?

It's not that I didn't get it. She is a single mom with two little kids (seven and eight at the time). She had security at her job. She was making a fantastic living.

I wanted Meg on my team, so I forced myself to flex my empathy muscles. How, you might ask? Well, it turns out that through some anatomical anomaly the empathy muscle starts at your brain, flows through your mouth, heads toward your eardrums, and ends right back in your brain. What I mean is that the more you consider another person's point of view, listen to what's being said, and articulate your thoughts back to that person, the easier it will be to do so in the future. Like all muscles, the more you use them the stronger they become. And, like other muscles, you start using them without even having to think about it.

So how did empathy work in our case?

ESTABLISH VALUE

I decided that Meg—her complementary personality, her expertise, and her work ethic—was worth the wait. I knew that it would drive me a little bit mad, but because of her value to me it was obvious that I needed to empathize with her during this massive transition in her life.

COMMUNICATE

I talked to her a lot and actually asked her those questions above when they swirled through my brain from time to time.

LISTEN

I listened to what she had to say. She decided to stick around her J-O-B for a big bonus that she had already earned, but wouldn't be awarded for three more months. In her mind, that was worth waiting for, and I had to honor that.

HOLD ACCOUNTABLE

I also established boundaries. How long would I wait? What was the limit of my empathy? After all, empathy without accountability always results in disaster.

We kept talking. All the time. About everything. It served us well, allowing us to continue to grow as a team and develop our IP. Not only did communicating help me empathize with Meg, but it also provided me with enough support to continue to carry forward on my own until she came on board full-time, five months after November 20th.

There is something that stands in the way of using empathy as a strategy, called the "negativity bias." It sounds like:

She's doing this just to make me mad.
He's so lazy, why can't she just stop procrastinating and get this done?
My boss hates me. I should just quit.

The negativity bias states that humans are predisposed to pay more attention to negativity as opposed to positivity. That means that negative thoughts, emotions, or social interactions have a more significant effect on our psychology than neutral or positive things.

According to Paul Rozin and Edward Royzman, psychologists at the University of Pennsylvania, negative experiences are dominant to positive ones. When humans combine positive and negative events or items, they tend to have an overall negative impression.

While we may be predisposed to a negative inner monologue, it doesn't have to rule our lives. We can reframe our internal message. Instead of agonizing over self-doubt, we can use that energy to program our thoughts to respond positively.

The first step is to pay attention. Simply being aware of when you're letting your negativity bias dictate how you feel about work or other people is the only way to change it. Once you realize you have a bias, you can start building habits, reactions, and thoughts that are positive.)

A helpful tool to reprogram the negative inner monologue created by the negativity bias is the Experience Cube, created by Gervase R. Bushe. In becoming aware of the four elements of the Experience Cube, you can start to separate what you're actually experiencing from the judgements and inferences you make in any given situation.

Observations: Sensory data, including what you see and hear. This includes facts about a situation: *w*hat actually occurred.

Thoughts: The meaning you add to observations. Thoughts are the way in which you interpret an experience.

Feelings: Your emotional or physiological response to the thoughts and observations. How do you feel?

Wants: The desired outcome. After processing an experience, what do you want out of it?

194

Let's pretend you just had a poor performance review from your boss.

You make the following **observation**:
I made an error on a report and was informed of it. My boss offered criticism, which is part of her job. Mark made a similar mistake last year and suffered no major consequences.

Based on the observations you've just made, you have this **thought**:
I'm going to get fired, I know it. I really screwed up those reports. It's not like other people don't screw up, too, but I'm the one who always gets noticed for it.

Then you have another, even worse, **thought**:
My boss thinks I'm an idiot. She'll never think that I qualify for a promotion. I'm a better fit for her job, anyway—she's jealous.

You are now drowning in negative **feelings**:
I'm humiliated, maybe I should just quit.
I'm so angry I can't even focus on my work anymore.

As you begin to separate your thoughts and feelings from your observations, you'll notice what a stretch from the truth (if not dead wrong) your interpretation is. Not only are these thoughts and feelings not based in reality, but they are also emotionally charged. Focus on your observations of a situation until your emotions can be wholly interpreted later, when you're calm.

Instead of thoughts and feelings, use your observations to interpret your **wants**:

I want a promotion, and in order to do that I need to meet the company standards. I need to improve in certain areas and should focus on those.

My aspirational goal is as follows: I want to make $80k next year with good benefits, while working for a company that is transparent and ethical.

If you are ever operating in a negativity bias, go back to your observations, and separate those observations from thoughts and feelings. Once you do, it's easy to see how a negative interaction can turn into a positive one:

One small error is not indicative of my work as a whole. If others have made a similar mistake and not suffered detrimental consequences, it's doubtful that I will.

I am not far from meeting the company's standards and getting a promotion. Today was a minor setback, and because my boss informed me of it right away, I can improve it.

If this company can get me to my aspirational goal, then I will work harder to ensure I have a place in it. If this company does not meet my criteria, then I have made a valuable discovery and will make a change.

When we learn to compartmentalize our observations, thoughts, feelings, and wants, we set ourselves up for interpreting raw data, rather than biased assumptions. Once a person begins reframing their internal message, you'll find that you are much more realistic in your concerns, more in touch with reality, and ultimately kinder to yourself.

LEARNICATE

"You can't expect your team to blindly follow your leadership if you haven't bothered to invest any time getting to know them."

Carey D. Lohrenz
The US Navy's first female F-14 Tomcat Fighter
Pilot and author of Fearless Leadership

One of our favorite strategies for not only employing empathy, but also for increasing accountability and strengthening communication channels across the board is a process Meg calls Learnicating.

Meg's Take:

If you are an enthusiastic participant, you might be a chronic interrupter. Maybe you interject because you think your colleague is moving in the wrong direction, and you don't want to waste time. Sometimes you interrupt to give your answer to your own question—maybe you are impatient and are just excited to share your own thoughts. Whatever the reason, you find yourself making corrections and interjections constantly. You take the reins on every conversation and steer it in the direction that you want it to go. I used to be a chronic interrupter, too. Then I realized I was sending the wrong message.

Growing up in rural South Dakota, I had to vie for my spot in the world as something other than a rancher. Even as a kid I felt like I had to prove that I not only desired, but was also capable of attaining something different than the people around me who were marrying young and working the land. I knowingly and unknowingly created an image of myself that was perpetually at odds with the expectations of those around me.

It wasn't always easy to keep that vision alive. Whenever I felt someone challenging it, I knew I had to push back even harder. In doing so, I created a construct of myself by which I always had to be right about everything. That construct allowed me to build confidence and work through a lot of external negativity and internal self-doubt. However, there were some unforeseen consequences of ensuring my point was heard across the board. For example, I interrupted everyone, a lot.

When I changed social circles in college I no longer needed to be the loudest voice in the room—everyone could finally hear me just fine. The need for my construct lessened, but the habits formed during that time stuck around. (Aside from Rachel: Meg still thinks she's right about **everything**! Ha!)

I noticed people start to disengage with me during a conversation and acquiesce to my point-of-view, even if I knew they didn't agree with it. I wondered what it was that they wanted to say and wondered why they were keeping silent. Eventually, I realized that interrupting people communicated these things:

I don't believe you.

I'm listening to respond.

I don't value your opinion.

I don't have time to hear you.

Not only is that not how I feel personally, but as a member of leadership that's a dangerous impression to give. Interrupting stifles discourse, effectively suffocating the opportunity to brainstorm and problem solve. One-sided communication ruins the relationship leadership has with their team, destroys new ideas, and fails to allow airtime for issues.

Today, I learn first and communicate second, or Learnicate. The first step in the Learnicate process is to take notes. I love having people burst through my door, saying,

"I have an idea!"

I now respond, "I need a pen and paper."

"Oh no, it's something small it will only take a second."

"So will grabbing some paper, just hold on." I pull out that pen and paper anyway. It's not because I couldn't remember what they said, it's because writing things down is an excellent way of ensuring that I'm listening instead of talking. If I'm in a group, I find the nearest whiteboard or flipchart.

When you write down people's ideas they can view and correct your interpretation. Their intended point becomes the record, rather than your own impression of it. Next time you are having a meeting with your team, formal or informal, grab the nearest whiteboard and start writing down everyone's concerns, comments, and critiques. If appropriate, take a picture of the whiteboard afterward and email it to everyone. Team members can then see the evolution of the discussion and can add things that were overlooked.

The second step in the Learnicate process is to ask clarifying questions. I started out by forcing myself to ask just one, measly question during a conversation. Now, I find that I can't go an entire conversation without asking questions. Showing curiosity makes the person you are talking with feel valued, and I, in turn, end up appreciating the discussion so much more than I would have if I was blindly asserting my own ideas.

Whenever Rachel and I are sitting in an audience, we are dumbfounded by how few people ask questions at the end. We can't believe that people can sit through a presentation on something that they are interested in or affected by (why else would they be there?) and at the end not have a single question to ask. Why?

Earlier this year, my daughters and I were watching Brain Games, a TV series "designed to mess with the ultimate supercomputer," your brain. This particular episode demonstrated just how much humans hate to be wrong. On the show, NPR Science Correspondent Shankar Vedantam introduced a phenomenon called the "illusion of knowledge." Vedantam describes it as follows: "Our brain is wired to try and provide an answer. It's a basic survival mechanism to make you feel more in control...even though you likely don't know how things work, your brain thinks it does. Your brain would rather pretend it knows something than admit it doesn't."

So, geographically savvy reader, how many countries are in Africa? Seriously, pull out a pen and paper and write down a high answer and a low answer.

What's your guess? My girls and I wrote down 30-50 and patiently waited for Vedantam to give the answer. I'm betting your response was somewhat close to ours (unless you're a geo-nerd like Rachel, who might actually know the answer).

"There are 54 countries in Africa."

Dang!

However, Vedantam points out that 54 isn't the only acceptable response. Not even close! There was no limit set to how high or how low we could answer, so why didn't we just guess 1-100? Or 1-1,000, just to be sure? 1-1 million and we'd still get it right, and we would have eliminated the possibility of error. Our brains trick us into being precise and accurate, even when it means being precisely accurate in our incorrectness. Humans are inclined to pretend that we know something and consistently get the wrong answer, instead of admitting we don't have a clue. That's why we didn't answer 1-1,000 and why people don't ask enough questions—they don't want to be wrong. That fearful mentality can sabotage us. Or, as Confucius said, "The man who asks a question is a fool for a minute, the man who does not ask is a fool for life." Without the confidence to ask questions, leadership will find themselves in the trap of perpetual "not knowing."

Forcing yourself to take the Learnicating approach will unleash your curiosity—about people, the way they do things, the way they think. Listening to and carefully documenting what another person is saying, and then asking a series of clarifying follow-up questions will give you an incredible ability to understand, empathize, and open yourself up to new ideas. Of course, you can't Learnicate unless you have established the trust to have a candid conversation. One way to encourage the kind of discourse that allows leadership to Learnicate is to walk the floor.

Whenever we ask a team what would make them happier at work, the number one thing we hear said a million different ways is, "I want to see more of the organization's leaders." When we relay that sentiment back to management, they will often say something like, "We know, we know, we just don't have time," or "We have an open-door policy!" An open-door policy lets leadership feel good about providing a mechanism that allows their people to interact with them without impeding on their schedule. The problem is employees rarely feel comfortable using it.

At a company we've worked with, leadership and HR were located on the second floor while the rest of the staff was either on the first or working in another location on campus. Everyone on the second floor had an open-door policy and a lot of them earnestly took the policy to heart, yet the employees still called the stairs to the second floor the "green mile" (meaning the long walk to certain and horrible death). They hated coming to the second floor just to discuss something with payroll, let alone to give feedback or make suggestions to leadership.

We suggested to better use the open-door policy, leadership should walk the floor. It's one thing to sit in an office with an open door and take a few seconds to imagine what a team is experiencing. It's another thing entirely to physically leave the office and see what the team's day-to-day looks like. Not only does it make leadership more approachable, but when their team brings a problem to their attention they know what their team is describing and therefore have a better chance of brainstorming a solution.

Walking the floor also allows leaders to schedule informal meetings with staff. It gives leaders an opportunity to engage at their convenience, making them accessible to their team and more receptive to suggestions. Increased communication in this way also establishes rapport. It helps leaders earn the trust of their team—no one is going to offer up suggestions or talk freely about problems until leadership has walked the floor a few times.

Furthermore, chatting in person with staff sends a much better message than a generic memo sent out by admin. Walking the floor makes two statements true: "I actually care," and "I want to understand." This time gives a team the opportunity to clarify roles and responsibilities, offer up new ideas and criticism, and engage with leadership. It gives leadership the opportunity to Learnicate.

Many influential leaders are making themselves more accessible to their staff. They are adopting a "flat" communication system, as opposed to the traditional "command/control." Michael Bloomberg, co-founder, CEO, and president of Bloomberg LP doesn't have a private office. Instead, he sits at a desk that is the same as everyone else's, smack dab in the middle of the floor. Zappos CEO Tony Hsieh has a similar communication style. His desk is the same desk that is given to new employees at the company's call center. That's because Zappos is building an environment where employees are encouraged to form close communication systems. "Close" refers to both communication style and proximity—employees have about 70 square feet to themselves.

How can a leader expect their team to leave their desk, walk that "green mile," and initiate communication if leadership isn't willing to in the first place? Walk over to someone you haven't talked to in a while and ask how they are doing. Ask another person how their work is coming along. Give employees individualized praise for work that they have actually done or are currently doing. Take the lead and be the first to break down the employee/management communication barrier. iX Leaders lead by example.

OWN YOUR iX

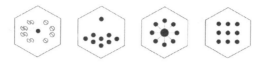

Here's the deal.

- Corporate success depends on the people within the organization.

- People's performance, energy, and commitment are directly impacted by their iX.

- iX is designed, either by accident or intention.

iX designed by accident is the kind of iX where teams show up to do the bare minimum, if they show up at all. Projects are rarely finished on time, unspoken conversations ruin teams, productivity plummets, and people abandon the organization. Leaders complain that they can't get anything done and wonder why their people act like they don't care. Team members can't figure out why leadership is so out-of-touch and wish they had a voice. Changes rarely stick, teams aren't cohesive, Monday is the worst day of the week, and the entire building drains the life out of anyone who steps foot inside.

AAHHHH!
Sounds awful, right? Maybe familiar, too?

What an exceptional iX means to *you*.

For Leaders: Imagine that tomorrow when you step through the front door of your office you find high, positive energy in the room.

Your team is excited and engaged. They are working together and holding each other accountable, giving you more time to focus on your own work, strategies, and goals.

As you walk the floor and connect with your people, you find that they are eager to talk about their work and are quick to offer relevant criticism. You realize your team is proactively seeking solutions, and can't remember the last time someone came running to you with a crisis—you and your team meet challenges head on before they turn into huge problems.

Whether you are an order-tolerant or chaos-tolerant leader, you know that your team will come through a boring or hair-on-fire day with competence, transparency, and a GSD attitude.

For Staff: Imagine that tomorrow when you sit at your desk you feel recharged and energized. It's not just you—the entire team feels it, too. You relax, knowing that leadership won't be breathing down your neck, believing that hiring great people means letting them decide the best way to get work done, be they order-tolerant or chaos-tolerant.

Not all days are fun—work is still work—but even the tough challenges are met with a GSD attitude. That's what exceptional iX provides: an environment where everyone can thrive, which allows for aspirational goals to be turned into already-dones, with the team's eyes set on the horizon to the next big thing.

iX designed with intention through iX Leadership will change the way everyone views company culture. We say everyone, because there has never been a company that hasn't needed some iX Leadership. In every vertical we've worked, in every size of business, in corporations, nonprofits, or privately held companies, everyone can benefit from designing their company culture. It will refocus leadership on their most valuable asset: their team. In doing so, the organization will create a culture where their people feel valued, empowered, creative, and energetic. Their team will go the extra mile not because they are told to, but because they *want* to. The energy that iX Leadership gives its people produces the kind of results that thought-leaders have been discussing for decades: increased sales, adherence to deadlines, retention, productivity, growth, and profit. iX Leaders create teams that don't just meet the bottom line, but continuously exceed it.

For iX Leaders, implementing change is…fun (yes, fun!). In your renewed company culture, initiatives consistently resonate across the board, and innovation courses through the veins of your organization. You and your higher-preforming teams leverage the Innovation Phase to achieve exciting new goals. You confidently hire the right new staff and place them in the right role, the first time. They meld with the rest of the team and buy into your vision. Your colleagues often ask how you get such consistently great work out of your team without standing over their shoulders. You smile to yourself, unable to remember the last time you were accused of micromanaging.

Leaders can no longer afford to leave iX to chance, it's simply too valuable. iX Leadership isn't just for companies that are struggling, but for companies that are doing "fine", "great", "okay" or "don't have problems." Even if the bottom line is black, it doesn't mean that a company is providing an awesome place to work. It also doesn't mean that company couldn't be more profitable.

Why stop at good when you can exceed great?

YOUR NEXT STEPS

Executive Leaders: The iX of your business is your responsibility. Get your internal leaders and change makers certified in iX Leadership, so they can develop an exceptional iX in the image of what you want to achieve. It's the only way it's going to happen.

Mid-level Leaders: You have the challenge of being in the middle of the org chart. You communicate between executives, your colleagues, and your staff. You see the big disconnects in Culture Types and Change in every direction. Get your iX Leadership Certification, so that you can use all of the amazing ideas, skills, and tools in this book on the regular. Make your life easier every single day. If you can't get your executive leadership bought in, don't be afraid to go guerilla-style. Create change where you are, where you can.

Front-line Supervisors: This might be your first leadership job, and you're likely struggling with where to even start. Start with an iX Leadership Certification. You'll learn basic leadership skills to help you avoid making common mistakes the first time. You'll also be able to figure out the Culture Types of everyone around you to better understand how you and your teams work. Then, when new challenges arise, you'll be able to handle them with confidence and skill. Higher-ups will complement you on your perceptive insight into how your people tick.

Staff/Employees/Boots on the Ground: You feel the pain of a poorly designed company culture—perhaps more than any other group in your organization. You see how disconnected leadership is. You feel like just a number. You are directly impacted by the consequences of too much change, too quickly. Take control of what you can. Get certified as an iX Ambassador or iX Leader to gain further insights and skills to manage tough situations with leadership and co-workers. Rely on a year of support from RGI to make your work life better.

Consultant, Trusted Advisor, Professional Service Provider, Salesperson: Become a Certified iX Ambassador and learn how to integrate Culture Types into your everyday professional life. Culture

Types will help you understand how well your clients will take on new ideas and big changes (even when it's their own idea). Independents might want to run ahead before you're ready for them to. Stabilizers may take six months to take on new processes. Know what to expect so you can better craft programs, implement strategies, and create sales approaches that resonate with the people your serving.

BE A PART OF SOMETHING BIG

iX Ambassadors and iX Leaders are members of the iX Community (https://ixleadership.com). Together, we will change the lives of 1 million people by the end of 2019. Get connected and stay excited about this epic goal. Whether you change 1 life or 1,000 lives, your contribution is counted and valued.

Why 1 million people? We don't play small.

This is our life's work—we are Fixers! We are committed to revolutionizing how leaders view the energy of their people. And, we need you—every Stabilizer, Organizer, Fixer, and Independent. You have valuable perspectives and motivations. Together, we will change the way business is done.

Can you feel it, too?!? The time is now. Be counted. Change the world. Join us!

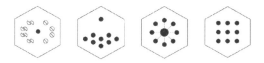

NOTES

iii   "To boldly go where no man has gone before" appeared in the original *Star Trek* science fiction television series. The complete introductory speech, spoken by William Shatner at the beginning of each episode, reads: "Space: the final frontier. These are the voyages of the starship Enterprise. Its five-year mission: to explore strange new worlds. To seek out new life and new civilizations. To boldly go where no man has gone before!" The phrase has since changed to the gender-neutral "where no one has gone before". The original *Star Trek* was Directed by James Goldstone and written by Samuel A. Peeples. "Where No Man Has Gone Before" aired on September 22, 1966.

6   The information on the Navy SEAL's stance on teamwork can be found in multiple articles, from multiple sources. This specific entry came from "Teamwork and Mental Toughness: More Important than Fitness, But..." by Stew Smith posted on Military.com in 2018.

7   The Caterpillar information was found in an excellent data-driven book called *The Best Team Wins*, by Adrian Gostick and Chester Elton. The authors cited the information from a report entitled, "The DNA of Engagement" by Rebecca Ray, Patrick Hyland, David Dye, Joseph Kaplan, and Adam Pressman. 2014.

7   We found the data on HK Metalcraft from a case study done by NJMEP, a private, not-for-profit organization that improves the profitability and competitiveness of New Jersey's manufacturers. The case study was entitled, "Soft Skills Produce Solid Results for Metalforming Manufacturer" and was published on December 3, 2013.

7-8   Gallup's landmark survey, "State of the American Workplace" delivers "analytics and advice on the changing workplace, using data collected from more than 195,600 U.S. employees, more than 31 million respondents, and insight from advising leading Fortune 1000 companies." It can be downloaded for free at Gallup.com. February 2017.

8   *Office Space* is a 1999 film written and directed by Mike Judge, and is absolutely hilarious.

8   In a UK article posted on ReviseSociology.com, researcher(s) found that "expressed as terms of a percentage of your life, 39.2 hours a week is spent working…[that is] equivalent to:

- 14% of your total time over the course of a 76 year period (based on the average projected life expectancy of 76 for people born in the year 2000 according to the ONS's National Life Tables for the United Kingdom.)
- 23.3% of your total time during the course of a 50 year working-life period.
- 21% of your total waking hours over a 76 year lifespan, assuming 8 hours of sleep a night.
- 35% of your total waking hours over a 50 year working-life period assuming 8 hours of sleep a night.
- 50% of your total waking hours during any given working day."

9   The CAP study referenced is called, "There Are Significant Business Costs to Replacing Employees" by Heather Boushey and Sarah Jane Glynn and was published on November 16, 2012. The SHRM estimate was found in an article entitled, "Financial Wellness: Is it worth the work?" published by Enrich.org.

11   The Katzenbach Center found in a 2013 survey that 44 percent of participants reported not understanding the changes they were expected to make, and 38 percent said

they didn't agree with the changes. The Katzenbach Center is a consulting agency specializing in organizational culture, teaming and informal organization.

15   Personality profile systems like Myers-Briggs Type Indicator®, DiSC®, Color Code®, and the 34-aspect StrengthsFinder® are all based off the work of Carl Jung, the founder of analytical psychology. Our typology, Culture Types, is also based on Jung's groundbreaking work. The difference is that rather than measuring personality, we measure a person's tolerance for chaos and how they work in a team. This makes Culture Typing especially valuable in an organizational context.

15   We read the statistic of "80% of employees' days are spent working on teams" originally in *The Best Team Wins*, by Adrian Gostick and Chester Elton. They found the statistic in "Collaborative Overload," by Rob Cross, Reb Rebele, And Adam Grant. Published in *Harvard Business Review*, January-February 2016.

17   Susan Cain's *Quiet: The Power of Introverts in a World That Can't Stop Talking* is often cited as a reversal in the way society viewed introverts. The article we accessed is entitled, "Susan Cain Instigates a 'Quiet Revolution' of Introverts" by Laura M. Holson in NYTimes.com, published July 25, 2015.

31-32   In Episode 1,101 of "Mister Rogers' Neighborhood" Mister Rogers shows viewers a film about fish before deciding to look at the fish in his own aquarium. When doing so he notices a dead fish laying at the bottom of his tank. Mister Rogers carefully removes the fish and attempts to revive it with salt water. Unfortunately, the fish has expired. Mister Rogers uses a paper towel to wrap the fish up, and prepares to bury it in his backyard.

32   A video of and accompanying article on Fred Rogers making his famous speech on behalf of PBS to President

Nixon and the U.S. Senate Subcommittee can be found in an article entitled, "The Best Argument For Saving Public Media Was Made By Mr. Rogers In 1969," written by Maxwell Strachan and published by HuffingtonPost.com on March 16, 2017.

35   *Breaking Bad* is an American neo-Western crime drama television series created and produced by Vince Gilligan and aired for five seasons on AMC. It was originally released in 2008. Quentin Tarantino's *Pulp Fiction* (1994) has become a cult classic.

39-41   Sharon Christa McAuliffe (September 2, 1948 – January 28, 1986) was an American teacher from Concord, New Hampshire, and was one of the seven crew members killed in the Space Shuttle Challenger disaster. The information on and quotes by Christa McAuliffe were taken directly from a transcript of "CNN PRESENTS Christa McAuliffe: Reach for the Stars" that aired January 22, 2006. A synopsis and discussion on McAuliffe and the Challenger explosion can be found in a video called "Christa McAuliffe – Full Episode" on Biography.com.

41-42   The Mine Health and Safety Act (MSHA) information was retrieved from an article entitled "History of Mine Safety and Health Legislation" published on MSHA.gov, and "Mine Fatalities – 100 Years of Progress" by Kyle Cramer and published by Mine Safety Center, updated December 15, 2015.

48-49   The Bill Gates profile was created from multiple sources. The comment about his questions getting continually more difficult to answer came from an article called, "The 4 Great Stories About Bill Gates That Show What It Was REALLY Like To Work With Him" by Julie Bort, published by Business Insider on August 23, 2014. The comment about Gates' feelings toward Excel was found in an article called

"PCs, Peripherals, Programs, and People" by and published in Byte Magazine in September 1985. "Bugs in Radio Shack TRS-80 Model III: How Bad Are They?" by Paul Freiberger and published on August 31, 1981. The comment about Gates studying a game until he solved the puzzle was taken from an interview entitled "Fred Thorlin: The Big Boss at Atari Program Exchange" Interviewed by Kevin Savetz and published by Atari Archives. Archived from the original on January 1, 2013. The characterization of Gates as being detail oriented was gleaned from a blog called "My First BillG Review" by Joel Spolsky, published on Joel On Soft-Ware on June 16, 2006. Finally, the intention of Bill and Melinda Gates to give away 95% of their wealth to charity was found in a BBC news article as well as "Briefly Noted | Excellence in Philanthropy | The Philanthropy Roundtable" published by philanthropyroundtable.org. Archived from the original on February 11, 2016.

56, 62   The SpaceX mission statement, to "revolutionize space technology, with the ultimate goal of enabling people to live on other planets" was taken directly from their website at SpaceX.com. SpaceX also directly published the statements about it's success in spacecraft engineering, writing "[SpaceX is] the only private company capable of returning a spacecraft from low Earth orbit, which it first accomplished in 2010. The company made history again in 2012 when its Dragon spacecraft became the first commercial spacecraft to deliver cargo to and from the International Space Station.

SpaceX successfully achieved the historic first reflight of an orbital class rocket in 2017, and the company now regularly launches flight-proven rockets. In 2018, SpaceX began launching Falcon Heavy, the world's most powerful operational rocket by a factor of two. missions as far as the

Moon or Mars…Building on the achievements of Falcon 9 and Falcon Heavy, SpaceX is working on a next generation of fully reusable launch vehicles that will be the most powerful ever built, capable of carrying humans to Mars and other destinations in the solar system." The conversation between host Chris Anderson and Gwynne Shotwell about working with Musk and SpaceX came from a transcript of a Ted2018 interview entitled, "SpaceX's plan to fly you across the globe in 30 minutes," published on Ted.com.

62-63 The opinion about new hires from traditional backgrounds was inferred by analyzing reviews from Tesla employees. One employee stated on Reddit, "It takes a certain type of personality to work at Tesla and I have seen many people come in wide-eyed and full of passion only to be seen leaving months later disappointed and burnt out. Not disappointed in the company, but more-so burnt out at the amount of energy required to work here. I have seen incredibly qualified associates be passed up on for a promotion who definitely deserved recognition. In which the promotion went to an outside hiring of individuals who have never had any experience in the car business being thrown directly into managerial positions." Glassdoor.com has 1,551 reviews on working for Tesla, with 116 calling it a "Fast-paced moving environment if you're the type who likes change," with many reviews calling Tesla innovative, but find it hard to maintain a work-life balance.

63-64 The story of Westergren and Pandora was found in an article called "How Pandora's Founder Convinced 50 Early Employees to Work 2 Years Without Pay" by Sam Parr, published by The Hustle on June 9, 2015. By following the link below you can hear his speech for yourself:

https://thehustle.co/how-pandoras-founder-convinced-50-early-employees-to-work-2-years-without-pay

73   Steven Amiel is the Chief Revenue Officer at Adler Branding & Marketing. He is responsible for developing and building the direct sales and channel relationships for Snappsearch, the only patented ad technology that enables users to search and receive results directly within the ad unit.

74   Elizabeth Purvis is a mentor for women and Creatrix of Feminine Magic® and Goddess Business School®.

75   The Stanford University study "Pressure and Perverse Flights to Familiarity" was done by Ab Litt, Senia Maymin, Taly Reich, and Baba Shiv and published in *Psychological Science* in 2011, Vol. 22, Issue 4, Pages 523-531.

77   "Habit" The American Journal of Psychology, by Andrews, B. R. (1903) published by the University of Illinois Press.

80   Famous Failures: We got our info on Colonel Sanders from an article called "Everything You Don't Know About The Real Colonel Sanders" by Venessa Wong, published on BuzzFeed on July 9, 2015. In 1954, just two years before Elvis's his big break he auditioned for a gospel quartet called the Songfellows. He was rejected. Read about it in an article called, "10 Interesting Facts About Elvis Presley" at ElvisDaily.com, May 3, 2016. In the New York Times Obituary Sarah Boxer writes that the "cartoons [Charles M. Schulz] drew for his high school yearbook were rejected." Schulz died at 77 on February 14, 2000. Milton Hershey failed twice before Hershey's chocolate. In 1876 Hershey started a confectionery business. His mother's family helped by subsidizing the business at first. After six years of hard work, the business went bankrupt in 1882. Hershey then went to Denver to work with a local confectioner, where he learned how to make caramels with fresh milk. Armed with

214

this new formula he soon left Denver to seek out opportunities in Chicago and New Orleans. Finding nothing he was drawn to New York City in 1883. There he started a second business. While this venture enjoyed some initial success, it also was plagued with cash flow problems and failed by 1886. Read more at www.hersheyarchives.org.

81   We've had quite a few conversations with Jeffrey Hayzlett about failure, change, and innovation through his Hero Club and the C-Suite Network. He kindly authored our foreword.

84, 119   We found this quote from Kettering in a great article called "The Failure-Tolerant Leader" by Richard Farson and Ralph Keyes. It was published through the *Harvard Business Review,* and can be found in the August 2002 Issue.

96   Dr. Rachel MK Headley created the Kurtz Change Transition Model (KCTM)© in 2016. The KCTM is based off of George Davis's model, which was originally conceived thirty years ago. It is different in two significant ways. In Headley's KCTM graph, Let Go is a gradual phase rather than a decision point. Secondly, the KCTM shows an Innovation Phase, which is critical to understanding a leader's capacity to leverage opportunity in a transition.

98   The information on Monet was found in an article called "Impressionism: Art and Modernity" from MetMuseum.org, published in *The Met.*

99   Marie Curie is one of the most revered female physicists and is known for her discovery of radioactive metals including Radium and Polonium. Find out more from our source, an article entitled "Inventions and Inventors: Marie Curie" at www.inventionware.com. 2013-2014.

99   Read more about Miles Davis in "1959: The Most Creative Year in Jazz" by Nathan Holaway, published at www.allaboutjazz.com on April 8, 2015.

135   John P. Kotter's *Leading Change* (1996) revolutionized the way we review leadership and change. He was one of the first to understand that being able to adapt to a changing business climate is integral to success. Furthermore, he realized that there is a difference between surviving change and leading through change.

136   The portrait of Hamdi Ulukaya was written with the help of "Just Add Sugar: How an immigrant from Turkey turned Greek yogurt into an American snack food" by Rebecca Mead, published in *The New Yorker* in the November 4, 2013 issue, and "How Chobani's Hamdi Ulukaya Is Winning America's Culture War" by Rob Brunner and published by FastCompany.com on March 20, 2017. Ulukaya's net worth was found on Forbes.com

138   The information on Courtney Dauwalter was found in the podcast the *Joe Rogan Experience*, "JRE #1027 – Courtney Dauwalter". It's a great listen! The description of the course was found on www.moab200.com, the race results were found at www.ultrasignup.com/results_event.aspx?did=43733#id14 10471

143   A video of Jim Carrey's interview on The Opra Winfrey Show can be found on YouTube under "Oprah - Jim Carrey - Visualization Empowerment" and was Published to YouTube on July 31, 2014.

146   Cy Wakeman's video where she responds to a leadership issue is called "Great Leaders Work With the Willing l Life's Messy, Live Happy EP4" by Cy Wakeman, published on YouTube on December 21, 2017.

147   Disengagement is at 68 percent, according to a recent Gallup article, called "The Worldwide Employee Engagement Crisis" by Annamarie Mann and Jim Harter, published at www.gallup.com on January 7, 2016.

158   The "Personal Accountability Model" was created by Mark
        Samuel. We first saw it in *The Power of Personal Accountability:
        Achieve What Matters to You* by Mark Samuel and Sophie
        Chiche, November 2004. We've found it to be an incredibly
        helpful resource for maintaining personal accountability.

176-177 TINYpulse provides a weekly survey to over 300 companies
        around the world. After analyzing over 40,000 anonymous
        responses, they uncovered important workforce trends. We
        found the information about employee happiness from an
        article they published, entitled "7 Vital Trends Disrupting
        Today's Workplace: Results and Data from 2013
        TINYpulse Employee Engagement Survey" published on
        TinyPulse.com.

176   The information on Buffer was found in an article called
        "After disclosing employee salaries, Buffer was inundated
        with resumes" By Vickie Elmer of *Quartz*, published on
        January 24, 2014.

177   SumAll and transparency: read more from the article "Why
        This New York Tech Startup Makes Everyone's Salary
        Transparent" by Richard Feloni, published by Business
        Insider on July 21, 2014.

177   In a Forbes article called "Using Transparency To Build A
        Better Company" contributors Bill Fotsch and John Case
        briefly mention Apptopia's "bank of monitors".

177   You can read Zappos full values guide at
        www.zapposinsights.com and see Patagonia's map of textile
        mills at www.patagonia.com/footprint.html.

178   "America's Most Hated Companies" By Samuel Stebbins,
        Evan Comen, Michael B. Sauter and Charles Stockdale.
        Published at 247wallst.com on January 22, 2018.

178   The quote about Pandora's Box can be found in *Men
        Explain Things to Me,* By Rebecca Solnit and published by
        Haymarket Books on April 14, 2014.

184   The research on hatters came from *Columbia Encyclopedia* by Lagassé, Paul, published by Columbia University Press in 2008 and an article entitled "A study of chronic mercurialism in the hatter's fur-cutting industry," a Public Health Bulletin from May of 1937.

189   We originally learned about Non-Complementary Behavior from the podcast Invisibilia, in an episode called "Flip the Script" which you can hear here: https://www.npr.org/programs/invisibilia/485603559/flip-the-script. The cast aired on August 8, 2016. According to Chris Hopwood, associate professor of Psychology at Michigan State University and Director of the Michigan State University Psychological Clinic, Complementarity suggests that we tend to respond in a way that complements another person's actions. He wrote a great blog post for NPR.com called "Don't Do What I Do: How Getting Out Of Sync Can Help Relationships" in which he discusses Non-Complementarity. Published July 16, 2016.

194   In a study called "Negativity Bias, Negativity Dominance, and Contagion" researchers Paul Rozin and Edward B. Royzman hypothesize "that there is a general bias, based on both innate predispositions and experience, in animals and humans, to give greater weight to negative entities." It was published at journals.sagepub.com on November 1, 2001.

194-196 The Experience Cube was created by Gervase R. Bushe and appears in his book, *Clear Leadership: Sustaining Real Collaboration and Partnership at Work*. Published by Davies-Black, an imprint of Nicholas Brealey Publishing in 2010.

199   Brain Games was a family friendly TV series that aired in 2011, 2013-2016. It was hosted by Jason Silva and created by Jerry Kolber and Bill Margol. The specific episode we reference is "Episode 6", which aired May 5, 2013.

218

202   The commentary on Michael Bloomberg's office was found in an article called "Michael Bloomberg's Office Is ... a Cubicle?!" by Maer Roshan and published on HollywoodReporter.com on March 9, 2015.

202   The Zappos info came from an article called "Why Zappos CEO Tony Hsieh Sits At The Same Size Desk As His Call Center Employees" by Aaron Taube. It was published by BusinessInsider.com on October 21, 2014.

INDEX

GRATITUDE

We have run across many people in our work and travels and each one has given us a new perspective – some of you made the book! While we've changed names to protect the (not-so) innocent, you know who you are and thank you. Thank you for your contributions to our life, experience, research, and literature.

In these days of likes, connections, and adds, we would like to take a moment to acknowledge the folks that helped us get where we are with the book and the business in real time. You inspire us, support us, and buy us drinks.

To Michelle Stampe, in the words of Dr. Seuss, "Kid, you'll move mountains!" Of course, kid is no reflection of your ability as a writer or your uncanny wit. You are timeless (even if you didn't know who Mr. Rogers is) and already successful beyond your wildest dreams.

To Doug Murano, the first person who read our manuscript with no back story – and yay, you liked it! Thank you so much for your time, words of support, and critical insight. The book is better for it (and we loved having a Bram Stoker Award Winner on the team!).

To Sion Lidster, poet extraordinaire, without whom the book would never have seen the light of day.

To Karl Post, Elissa Wiese, Mike Edgette, and Seth Menacker (#winner!) who made sure the book was seen by more than our besties.

To Dr. Kracher, you sent me away from college with some great advice, again from Dr. Seuss, and I've lived by it faithfully for the last several years. I am who I am and your pushing me to never give up on myself has led me to book writing, taking on the challenge of changing the global business environment, and running marathons. I am honored to call you my mentor and friend. Thank you, sincerely and forever, for sharing your fervor with me. ~Meg

To Elizabeth Purvis, the business coach that set me on the path, who gave me permission to do what I needed to do, and who continues to inspire me to see beyond the horizon. Thank you for lighting the way. Mwah! ~Rachel

To Jeffrey W. Hayzlett: When we sit around the office debating strategy, we often say WWJWHD – What Would Jeffrey W. Hayzlett Do? Thank you for being an example of a true disruptor. And thank you for the Hero Club, without which our lives would be much less exciting.

To our Board of Advisors: Tricia Benn, George Brunt, Carol Greco, and Robert Steele. Thank you so much for your belief in our mission and our ability to pull it off. Your willingness to support RGI is delightful and humbling.

To Jo and Pete, from long work days in the office to days on the road to working from the city pool. You are my rock and my heart, and I couldn't have asked for a better team. Love, Mom.

To my witty, nutty, and amazing Alex: you are my pride, my hope, my future Supreme Court Justice. I love you, Kid. Love, Mom.

To Jared "Cappie" Capp, my oak tree: our life together is incredible, exciting, and fun. Thank you for our journey from Belize and beyond. Your unwavering support has lifted me ever higher, and I can't wait for tomorrow! ~Rachel

To Rich & Sherry, Peggy & Kelly, Cliff & Jeri (the folks): thank you for lighting the fire, so we may lead the way for others.

To Dr. Rachel MK Headley, holy shit, what a ride! Tears of joy, huffs of anxiety, travel delirium and arguments about priorities (where we were actually agreeing the whole time) brought us to ass-kicking, book-writing, game-changing Utopia. I can't wait to jump off the next cliff with you!   ~Meg

To Meg, there is nothing I enjoy more than creating business magic with you. I love our drive to help others, play big, and change the world. The joy we find together means more to me than you can ever know. Thanks for The Bucket (and the tears, laughs, and passion held within!). Onward! ~Rachel

Made in the USA
Lexington, KY
22 September 2018